The World of
The International Manager

The World of
The International Manager

An Introductory Text on the Nature
and Practice of Global Business

JOHN HUTTON

89-1594

Philip Allan

OXFORD and NEW JERSEY

First published 1988 by

PHILIP ALLAN PUBLISHERS LIMITED
MARKET PLACE
DEDDINGTON
OXFORD OX5 4SE (UK)

and

171 FIRST AVENUE
ATLANTIC HIGHLANDS, NJ 07716 (USA)

British Library Cataloguing in Publication Data
Hutton, John
   The world of the international manager.
   1. Multinational companies. Management
   I. Title
   658′.049

   ISBN 0-86003-559-X
   ISBN 0-86003-659-6 Pbk

Library of Congress Cataloging-in-Publication Data
Hutton, John, 1933—
   The world of the international manager.
   1. International business enterprises — Management.
   I. Title.
   HD62.4.H87   1988   658′.049   88—19412
   ISBN 0-86003-559-X
   ISBN 0-86003-659-6 (pbk.)

Typeset by MHL Typesetting Ltd, Coventry
Printed and bound in Great Britain by the Camelot Press, Southampton

Contents

Acknowledgements

The preparation of this book extended over a long period of time. Much of the original stimulation came from Sir James Lindsay when, as Director of International Studies at Henley, he conceived and ran the Directing International Operations programme during the 1970s. This attracted practising managers from multinational companies, international organisations and aid agencies, and from Eastern European and developing countries. All enjoyed a unique learning experience of living and working more effectively in the fast-changing global business scene. Included was a spouses programme, led by Lady Peggy Lindsay, which dealt with the particular problems of family life on an international scale. The need to enhance cross-cultural sensitivity and awareness was given particular emphasis and has shaped my own views on the world of the international manager since that time. Many other insights have come from a succession of fellow contributors and participants on subsequent international management programmes at Henley and elsewhere. It is impossible to list them all individually.

Among institutions, I would especially acknowledge helpful contacts over a long period of time with the Centre for International Briefing, Farnham Castle; the Royal College of Defence Studies and the former National Defence College, Latimer; the Department of Economics at Reading University; the Royal Institute of International Affairs at Chatham House; and the Commonwealth Development Corporation both at home and abroad. Mention must also be made of contacts with the Bureau of Public Enterprises, New Delhi, India; the Australian Administrative Staff College, Mount Eliza, Victoria, Australia; the International Business College at Ziest in the Netherlands; and the Centre de Perfectionnement aux Affaires, Jouy en Josas, France.

Individuals whom I would particularly thank include Mr David Stephen and his colleagues of the Commonwealth Development Corporation, London who, in 1987, gave up a day to discuss with me their own experiences of managing in developing countries. This followed on from earlier contacts with Dr David Marshall and other staff at the Mananga Agricultural Management Centre in Swaziland during two visits in 1985. This Centre provided much of the material for Chapter 7. Over the years much valuable help has also been received from Dr Michael Brooke, formerly Director of the International Business Unit at the University of Manchester Institute of Science and Technology; from Dr Richard Mayne, formerly head of the European Communities Office in London; and from Mr Michael Kaser, Professorial Fellow at St Antony's College, Oxford. My thanks must also go to many postgraduate research students, both at Henley and at Brunel University, notably Mr Robert Willis, formerly with the Economist Newspaper and now with Prudential Bache, who contributed substantially to Chapter 2. Many other ideas and comments were received from the members of the MBA programmes at Henley and Brunel and, recently, from the City University in London.

Amongst Henley colleagues Harry Slater, Bernard Taylor, Mike Jones, Malcolm Warner and Ysu Hu have all played their own distinctive parts.

Finally, may I take this opportunity of thanking Mrs Wendy Morris and Miss Margaret Drage for their work, so readily and carefully undertaken, in the preparation of the final manuscript for this book.

John Hutton
September 1988

Introduction

International business studies have an increasingly important part in the curricula of management and business studies programmes in schools, polytechnics and universities. It was not always so. Diplomats and military men have for long studied the world of global power balances and international relations as a basis for national security and defence. Today, international business managers must also learn how to monitor and respond to those global (market) forces which underlie the future growth, prosperity and survival of their enterprises.

Much of business today is truly global, with internationally produced goods and services being distributed and sold in increasingly competitive world markets. As the experience of the world's automobile industry shows, direct challenges to corporate profitability and survival no longer gradually emerge in overseas markets. As General Motors, Ford, Volkswagen, Fiat, Renault, Rover and many others have learnt to their cost, motor vehicles from Japan and other newly industrialising Far Eastern producers now present a massive direct challenge in hitherto secure home markets.

Similar global competitive forces can also be seen at work in many other markets as well. They have often appeared like a hurricane out of a blue sky, literally blowing away, in a brief space of time, the security and livelihoods of many unprepared companies and industries. Cries for protectionism have been heard throughout Western Europe, North America and Australasia to save local industries and markets, and the jobs threatened by the fierce winds of international competition, innovation and change.

The huge post-war growth in multinational businesses and markets therefore makes it essential that both aspiring and practising international managers must understand and respond to a far wider range of cultures, conditions and languages than before. A deeper understanding of widely different business environments, shaped by diverse religious backgrounds, nationalistic values and attitudes, has become an essential part of a manager's experience. He, or she, must be sensitive to the many other political, economic, social and technological changes which underlie the international scene. New market and investment opportunities and risks appear and disappear in many places and forms. For the international manager, they extend from the consumer-driven, affluent markets of the advanced Western industrial and urban countries and the newly in-dustrialising countries (NICs), to the scarcity-afflicted markets of the so-called 'developing world'. The Eastern socialist bloc countries of the COMECON group also provide other opportunities. Finally, the fluc-tuating fortunes of the oil-producing OPEC member states present yet a further instance of the opportunities and risks of 'boom-and-bust' global market conditions.

International managers, faced by such continual competitive challenge in the global market, must be adept at devising new corporate strategic responses and initiatives. They must be aware both of the changing needs of the hour, and the special requirements of specific market locations. They must maintain effective corporate global business strategies and market assessment procedures which are both responsive to, and capable of dealing with, opportunities and risks as and when they appear. Managers must be closely attuned to the nature of markets, and of those governmental and other institutions and regulations which impact on the ways in which business now functions, at both local and global levels. Production and distribution systems, sales, marketing and pricing policies all need to be tailored to the needs of both international and local cir-cumstances. The reality of fluctuating currency exchange rates, and of intractable debt situations in many countries presents yet further challenges to managerial wisdom and ingenuity.

Finally, and by no means least, both the student and the practising manager and his family must be adequately prepared for the many acute challenges of living and working for long periods of time in countries, cultures and languages other than their own. This, in essence, is what the world of the international manager is all about. The purpose of this introductory textbook is to study these challenges which now apply to doing business successfully in all parts of the world.

1

Taking a Global Viewpoint

At the beginning of this century, an observer of the rapidly changing international scene penned the following lines in *The Business Blue Book* of 1905 about global events and their implications for managers. His view of the world at that time still has relevance over 80 years on.

> The enormous growth of the world's population, the progress of civilisation the world over, the wonderful and increased facilities for travel and transport, the strides made by foreign competitors into what were once our exclusive markets, the enormous growth of commerce and consequent extensive distribution of capital, all these happenings make it of the utmost importance that our commercial instincts should be cultivated by more liberal education, broader views and keener powers of observation. Travel will prove of the utmost advantage to the keen observer, by showing him the smallness of his knowledge and increasing his breadth of view.

1.1 An Historical Scenario

Later in the chapter we shall consider in detail the major strategic elements which make up the fast-changing global business environment, and which will go on exerting their influences into the 1990s and beyond. Before considering these important current and future issues, it is essential to have an idea of the historical development of the present system of international trade, finance and markets. Prior to the nineteenth century, three broad time phases have been identified:

(a) The first phase saw the formation and gradual development of the Western European nation states, and their commercial and military competition with each other. This was accompanied by their economic penetration of the remainder of Europe and their trading extension to many parts of the world outside Europe. During the

3

period, from approximately 1500 to 1700, the first colonial empires of Portugal, Spain, Holland, France and England were gradually extended, consolidated and established.

(b) A second phase led to the re-grouping of the remainder of Europe into a system of states; accompanied by the extension of political control into most parts of the non-European world. This phase occurred between approximately 1650 and 1850. The main exceptions to the rule were the ancient civilisations of China and Japan which remained substantially independent of European influence, up to the middle of the nineteenth century.

(c) A third phase, from the middle of the nineteenth century onwards, saw the extension of the European states' influence to the rest of the world; to the gradual granting of political independence to many former colonies; and through the uneven incorporation of powerful ancient societies like China and Japan into the international trading and financial system.

For much of the period before 1820 the practices of European based international trade and finance were dominated by the theories of *mercantilism*, which suggested that nation states would do best if they centred all power into their own hands and concentrated on expanding trade with their colonial possessions. However, these colonial trade protectionist policies were vigorously attacked by the British classical economists, notably Adam Smith (1723—90) and David Ricardo (1772—1823). The period from 1820 to 1870 saw the acceptance of more *laissez-faire* global trading philosophies, which in Britain led to an extension of a wider range of multinational trade relationships. The 1870s until the beginning of World War I in 1914 brought a 'Golden Age' of global trade. It saw the establishment of a huge network of world-wide inter-continental trade networks, often within colonial contexts. Yet it also saw the deterioration of many freer trade relationships, as Britain's emerging major industrial competitors — Belgium, Germany, France and the United States, developed new 'infant' industries and increasingly sought means to exclude British and other competitors from their domestic and colonial markets.

Throughout this century of major economic development and change, London developed a pivotal role in the world trading system, and became a huge source of savings for international finance. The adoption of sterling as a reserve trading currency linked to gold was of critical importance for the international financial standing of the United Kingdom, and for the smooth functioning of the global trading system.

World War I (1914—18) brought to a climax a century of global trade competition and colonial rivalries. The inter-war decades, from 1919 to 1939, saw a disintegration of the free trade spirit and the intensification of strong economic nationalism. It saw the adoption of 'beggar-my-neighbour' trade policies by the major European industrial nations, and an attempt by all to establish tied colonial trading relationships as the basis for their industrial economies.

In the case of Great Britain, the largest of the imperial powers, the 1931 trading agreements, known as the Commonwealth Preference System, represented a major attempt to link the primary producing members of the Commonwealth and Empire into a linked set of preferential commercial and financial relationships with Great Britain. Yet a number of former British colonies were beginning to industrialise rapidly. India, Australia, New Zealand, South Africa, Canada all took on greater industrial activity, which in many cases was financed and developed by British companies. These increasingly politically independent members of the British Commonwealth were looking for ways to develop their own industrial and trading powers, free from restraints of trade ties with Britain, the mother country. The United States also pursued a strong protectionist policy, anxious to protect and expand American industrial capacity and to link markets in South America and Asia to her own industrial interests. Japan was seen as a political rival and possible major trading competitor to the United States in the Pacific. In turn, the Japanese looked to the exploitation by military means of Manchuria and China, and to the development of a co-prosperity region of Asian markets linked to Japanese industry.

The international chaos and destruction of World War II (1939—45) swept many of these arrangements and attitudes into the dustbin of history. In 1944 the Bretton Woods conference led to the creation of the International Bank of Reconstruction and Development and the International Monetary Fund charged with promoting stability of world trade and acting as a global central bank. Later, in 1947, the General Agreement on Tariffs and Trade (GATT), originally signed by 23 countries, led to a gradual reduction of barriers and to harmonisation of world trade. The post-war era has seen a continuation of these trends with a host of international organisations, agreements and plans shaping the nature of the international business environment.

Figure 1.1 The Global Business Environment: Its Impact on International Markets

1.2 The Post-World War II 'Golden Age' of Growth

During much of the four decades after 1945 the global economy experienced a 'golden age' of growth, with agricultural and industrial production and trade far exceeding the levels achieved in any previous epoch. In the 1950s the British Prime Minister, Harold Macmillan, confidently told the British people 'You never had it so good'. Expansion of the world economy exceeded the growth of population, and average living standards rose significantly, particularly in the advanced urban and industrial countries. This post-war economic growth was assisted by a number of circumstances, not the least of which was the absence of major wars between the leading military powers. However, the Korean war of the early 1950s, and the wars in South East Asia from the 1940s and through to the 1970s had profoundly disturbing effects, as did the many other outbreaks of violence associated with the end of colonial rule and the struggles for power endemic in many territories. During the 1970s and 1980s the growth of terrorism on an international scale also became a de-stabilising element for international business opportunities.

For industry and trade, the post-war reductions of trade barriers under the General Agreement on Tariffs and Trade greatly assisted the processes of reconstruction and growth. The worldwide application of national economic demand techniques and policies, inspired by the work of the British economist, J.M. Keynes, coupled with the provision by the United States of its massive post-war current account surpluses to finance the reconstruction of war-devastated Western Europe and Japan, and to assist many of the developing countries, was also an important factor underpinning the growth in the 1950s and 60s of the global free market economy. Yet by the early 1970s, the break-up of the Bretton

Table 1.1 Some Global Issues in the 'OPEC Decade' of the 1970s

1. OPEC oil price rises:
   — quadrupling in 1973–74,
   — doubling in 1978–79,
   leading to:
2. Slower, less stable growth worldwide:
   — output 3 per cent per annum,
   — output per head 2 per cent per annum,
   — trade 6 per cent per annum.
3. Inflation, leading to:
   — loss of dollar convertibility to gold 1971.
4. Weakening of capital and consumer markets in many industrial countries.
5. Decline in investment returns in many industries.
6. Balance of payment problems for many countries.
7. Growth of new competition from newly industrialising countries.
8. Third World problems become more urgent:
   — population, food, debts, violence.
9. OPEC — recycling of oil surplus finances.
10. Widespread disenchantment with 'big' government (but was 'small' beautiful?).
11. Rapid *technological* changes with implications for employment on a global basis.

Table 1.2   Some Global Issues in the Uncertain 1980s

---

1. Energy availability and prices fluctuated.
2. Inflation rates and government policies varied widely.
3. Continued balance of payments problems for many OECD countries, notably the USA.
4. The growth of government debt — notably in the USA.
5. The trade threat from Japan and the newly industrialised countries continued.
6. Calls for protectionism intensified in USA, Western Europe, and elsewhere.
7. Domestic structural issues included:
    (a) static, ageing populations in industrial countries,
    (b) fewer jobs coming from new investments,
    (c) technological change and productivity impacted on employment and training needs,
    (d) market and capital saturation in many markets,
    (e) which way to grow increasingly preoccupied business planners in the advanced industrial countries.

Woods managed system of world finance led to monetary instability, great business uncertainty, and made the control of inflation world-wide difficult to achieve. The 1970s also saw the end of two decades of not only cheap but falling energy prices. From 1973 onwards, the so-called 'OPEC decade' became influenced by the impact of increasing and then sharply fluctuating energy prices which affected both the industrial and developing world. The same inflationary and de-stabilising forces were also associated with rising prices for many other basic materials and pro-ducts. The problem of re-cycling the surplus funds from the lower importing OPEC oil producing states, into creative new investments in both the industrial and developing world, became the major challenge for the world's financial system. The 1980s era of floating exchange rates and unpredictable currency flows has introduced even less stability in an often chaotic if increasingly interdependent global market economy.

1.3   World Politics and National Resources

Politically the world today is divided into some 180 or so separate and independent states, most of which have come into existence since the end of World War II and the withdrawal of the Western European powers from colonial rule. Over half of the world's present family of nations are former British colonies. While in international law all of these new states are sovereign, they differ hugely, both in the natural resources and populations which they contain, and the extent to which they are capable of asserting their interests in upholding their independence. At the top of the contemporary world hierarchy are the two super-powers, the USA and the USSR. To some extent, these are matched by the other states making up the European Community; by Japan, India, China, Canada, Brazil, Argentina, South Africa, and other industrialised or industrialising states. Under this top echelon of significant, if highly varied, industrial and urban societies are many other nations still largely dependent on their mineral or agricultural production. At the far extremity are many tiny states, such as Western Samoa and the Maldive Republic, which have only recently moved out of colonial status, have limited natural resources and small populations, and are dependent on subsistence agriculture, minerals and tourism for their livelihood.

Underlying the international status of all these politically independent states are such geographical considerations as the nature of topography, of location, size and shape, of climate and natural resources and population. Historical and cultural inheritances and social structures are also important in determining the way a nation is regarded by the world community. Economic factors relating to the production of natural resources, including basic energy, foodstuffs, manufactures and services, as reflected in the Gross National Product (GNP) and in per capita income, are important indicators of the standing of a nation in the global market scene. Linked to this is the critical pace of the rate of scientific and technological advance, and the ways in which such ideas are effectively applied in different countries to productive purposes.

There are in addition, diverse political factors, i.e. nationalism, forms of government, ideological and religious beliefs and national interests, etc. which make up a nation. There is also the question of the ability of any state to support its national interests and policies by the exercise of military and strategic forces. The Falklands episode, the Israeli incursion into Lebanon in pursuit of the PLO, the Iraq—Iranian conflict, the Soviet invasion of Afghanistan, the conflicts in central America, all illustrate the extreme diversity and instability of much of the contemporary global, political, religious and military scene.

The strategic global business question is whether *convergency* can ultimately mitigate the underlying tensions and conflicts of the modern world, or whether other *divergencies* will arise, with grave implications for the aspirations of continued economic and social advances for all. The interdependency of many aspects of the modern world makes an awareness of such issues of great importance for successful global market and investment planning, both now and in the foreseeable future.

1.4 Global Competition or Protectionism?

In the previous sections we have surveyed the main historical developments that have shaped our present global industrial trading and financial environment. All of these developments were influenced by, and in turn led to, the creation of theories and practices of competition or protectionism shaping the conduct of industry and trade on an international scale.

Monitoring developments and trends in world trade practices and developments remains a critical task for government officials and international managers. Since the end of World War II, the world's free trading economy was progressively liberalised under the influence of the GATT, the IMF, and other institutions. The global commercial environment changed even more after the Tokyo round of trade negotiations which was launched in September 1973, on the eve of the first oil crisis. The subsequent six years of negotiations took place against the increasing crises of rising prices for energy, balance of payments difficulties, monetary upheavals, inflation, unemployment and partial relapses into protectionism on the part of many countries. There were fears that the talks themselves might break down altogether. Yet new codes of conduct did finally come into force in 1980. These did not represent the great surge forward to a freer trading world which many had hoped for in the autumn of 1973. The body of protectionist measures surrounding agriculture — such as are embodied in the European Community's CAP (Common Agricultural Policy) and in US agricultural policies — were hardly tackled. Australia and New Zealand and the developing Third World countries were far from happy with the way that the leading industrialised countries consistently neglected their interests.

In the early 1980s retaliatory threats by the US government against 'subsidised' steel exports from EEC countries and an attempted American embargo on US multinational engineering exports to the Siberia—Europe gas pipeline were also illustrative of world trade tensions. The USA also threatened a global price war with what they regarded as subsidised European grain exports to major Third World markets. In turn, Australia launched a diplomatic and negotiating offensive against both the USA and the European Community for 'dumping' of grain on Third World markets.

All trade regulations and practices came under huge new pressures in the less expansive lower growth economic climate of the 1980s. The decade has certainly seen an aggressive search for new export markets by the traditional industrialised countries as their domestic growth rates weaken. These countries at the same time often exercised as much protectionism against competitive imports as they could get away with. Starting early in 1980, there was a modest eight-year tariff-cutting schedule, which the EEC reserved the right to review after five years. In the non-tariff sector it was not clear how many of these codes had worked out in practice, and there are still doubts about their legal status within GATT. Few developing countries signed the codes, the majority feeling that they were irrelevant to their needs. A further disappointment for the developing countries was the failure to reach any agreement on new safeguard procedures, though talks continued. If no new rules can be worked out, there is likely to be continuing conflict over interpretation of the existing GATT provisions and an increasing number of import limitation agreements concluded outside GATT.

Some of the new industrialising countries, like Brazil and India, are beginning to accept that, as they industrialise, they must shed some of the privileges they acquired when they were poorer. If they do not do this, the richer industrial countries will ultimately feel forced to close their markets to competitive imports from these sources. Japan is under strong pressure from both the USA and the EEC to open her domestic markets more comprehensively to products and services from overseas suppliers.

All these debates and conflicts will extend into the 1990s and as such will require continuous monitoring and action by both concerned government trade officials and international managers.

1.5 Britain within the European Community

Britain is but one example of a traditional, highly industrialised nation continually and often painfully adjusting to changing global conditions. Her present role in the world economy reflects both historical circumstances and deep cultural and political links. Foremost amongst the historial considerations is the inheritance of the great coal- and steam-powered Industrial Revolution of the late eighteenth and early nineteenth centuries. Cultural and political influences include the many world-wide links which the former colonial empire has bequeathed to present generations. The English language, laws and institutions have taken root in many other countries. They offer major potential advantages to English-speaking businessmen. The fact that America remained predominantly English-speaking was, as Bismarck, the nineteenth-century German Statesman observed 'the most significant development of the age'. Since the mid-1970s her proximity and long historical links with other Western European countries have also been reinforced by membership of the EEC. The move to even greater harmonisation of trade conditions and policies in 1992 indicates the force of this relationship.

Britain's present population of 56 millions constitutes about one-sixth of the total population of the expanded, twelve-nation European Economic Community of some 323 millions, but barely 1 per cent of the world's total. By the end of the century current demographic trends mean that Britain's population will be less than 1 per cent of the world's population. Still a major trading and industrial power, Britain today exports 8 per cent of world manufactures, compared to nearly 16 per cent a decade or so ago. With a high density of population to land area, she imports nearly half of her foodstuffs and most basic raw materials for industry. However, coal and, currently, North Sea oil and gas, together with nuclear technology, give the promise of energy self-sufficiency for many years to come.

Britain, in trying to maintain her global market and strategic political position, is confronted with the need to link the inheritance from the past with the needs of the present and the desired goals for the future. During the past 40 years Britain has moved from governing nearly a quarter of the world's population to a new relationship with the Commonwealth, and a close political, economic and social partnership within the still evolving European Economic Community. The political ideal of a 'special relationship' with the United States implies a high priority for the maintenance of the Atlantic Alliance, and for keeping the US commitment to the defence of Western Europe. Her NATO policy suggests the need to encourage partner states to take a 'balanced share' of defence costs, and to encourage a continuation of Western Europe's historical influence in international affairs, with Britain in a leading role. Attempts are also made to encourage continuing dialogue and, hopefully, a détente with the Soviet Union and the Warsaw Pact countries.

Britain has also sought to promote greater trade and cultural relations with the COMECON group as a whole though this has on occasion brought sharp diplomatic conflict with US policies. China's recent emergence in world affairs has led Britain, with other Western industrialised nations and Japan, to look for ways of seeking new export markets, to establish the agreement to transfer Hong Kong back to Chinese sovereignty in 1997, and also to use China as a counter to Soviet influence in Asia. There are continuing attempts to increase political, cultural and economic contacts with the formidable industrial competitor, Japan, to seek to establish a more balanced trade with that country, and to promote better relationships between Japan and the European Community as a whole.

Britain also maintains long-standing trading and financial links in Africa, not least of which is the fact that much of the West's strategic minerals comes from that great continent. The evolving situation in the southern half of Africa, focussing around the future of independent Zimbabwe and its relationship with other neighbouring states, notably the Republic of South Africa, takes a prominent part in the news headlines. There is also the critical question of diplomatic relationships with the other black African states, including Nigeria, which today takes a larger share of Britain's trade than goes to her former major trade partner, South Africa. Other needs are for Britain both to diversify and to continue to sustain her trade links with the nations of the Middle East, Latin America, Australasia, and South East Asia as a whole, since they still form an important part of the complex pattern of Britain's overseas diplomatic, trading and financial relationships.

*   *   *

Looking specifically towards relationships within Western Europe and in the evolution of the expanding European community, regular newsletters and publications from the European Communities office in London can provide managers with up-to-date information on the current position of the Community in the world. The idea of closer European political, economic and social unity was vigorously promoted in the post-war years by the French statesmen Jean Monnet and Robert Schumann (see Mayne 1983). The formation of the European Coal and Steel Community in 1952 and the Treaty of Rome in 1957 were crucial steps. Today the functioning of the Commission, the Council of Ministers, the European Parliament, the Court of Justice and the financing of the Common Agricultural Policy are everyday items of report and active debate. The fact that many trade relationships are negotiated on a Community-wide basis and that community laws influence business practices widely is also an important feature of the current global commercial scene.

The developing relationship between Britain and other industrial or industrialising states of the twelve-nation Community is an important element in global markets. Britain entered the Community in 1973—75 because she believed that membership provided the best means of safeguarding longer-term trade interests and of improving economic prospects. Britain's main political concern was that the strategic alignment of Western Europe and North America should be strengthened, and that her historic links with the Commonwealth should also be maintained. For British foreign policy, Winston Churchill's post-war conception of three circles — the Commonwealth, the United States and Western Europe — has remained a continuing element in its view of the world. Direct elections to the European Parliament may gradually alter this view. Yet, the persistence of national values and interests continues to bedevil attempts to create greater harmonisation and unity in Western Europe. Disputes about the working and efficiency of various Community institutions, of Britain's financial contribution to the Community budget and, especially, the Common Agricultural Policy, highlight but some of the issues involved.

During much of the 1970s there was widespread concern about Britain's lagging industrial performance putting a brake on the growth of the Community. However, improvements in the economy in the 1980s have suggested that British industry can adjust to the new realities. It is essential that its competitive capabilities *vis-à-vis* industry in Western Germany, France, Italy and Spain, etc. be sustained. Increased market harmonisation and competition from 1992 onwards also suggest further opportunities and challenges. Finally, closer industrial co-operation between European companies will also be of critical importance in maintaining competitive strength in global markets as a whole. Barclays Bank, plc and the EEC have published a booklet (1988), *Preparing for 1992*, which suggests a positive company strategy that should help in this process.

1.6   Some Global Scenarios for the 1990s

Business planners looking at global market opportunities for their companies' products and services need to consider short (1—3 years), medium (4—10 years), and long (10—30 years) scenarios. Plainly, many issues are specific to the particular nature of the products and markets surveyed. Some strategic industries are linked to energy, e.g. oil, coal, gas, nuclear, electricity, iron and steel, defence contracting, the motor industry, construction and building. The construction of major infra-structures such as dams and roads, bridges and airports requires very long lead times. The scale of these investments necessitates a more macro view of global market prospects.

(a) Studies of Scarcity, Wealth and Welfare

Numerous reports, books and papers have been prepared on the future of the world economy to the year 2000 and beyond. The long-term concern underlying all these studies of global *scarcity, wealth* and *welfare* is whether market growth can continue indefinitely: or must some improvements eventually come to an end, and a stationary state, or even absolute decline in average living standards be settled for? One famous speculation published in 1926 by a Soviet economist, N.D. Kondratieff, looked to long cycles of 30 years' economic upturn, which are then followed by 30 years' slower growth or even stagnation. For some observers the post-war 'Golden Age' of growth came to an end in the late 1960s and early 1970s and for the next two or three decades we are set for a lower rate of economic growth world-wide. It has also been suggested that these very long global market cycles inter-relate with and influence medium-term prospects. These medium-term activities include the so-called Kuznets 15–20 year capital investment cycles, (named after S. Kuznets, the first Nobel Prize winner in economics in 1971) and the still much shorter-term economic demand management policies, now followed in various ways by the governments of all the major Western industrial economies.

(b) OECD Interfutures Group

A report and series of working papers were produced in 1979 by the Interfutures Group of the OECD, an international team of experts led by Jacques Lesourne, called *Facing the Future, Mastering the Probable, and Managing the Unpredictable*. This report suggests that the global power balance between different nations and groups of nations will change substantially by the year 2000. It is envisaged that America's huge resources will ensure her remaining in the vanguard of the world's superpowers, but her relative political role may diminish because of a declining share of world income. At the same time, Japan's emergence as a major economic power, coupled with the industrialisation of South-East Asia and the growing strength of China, is likely to create an important world economic centre in the Far East by the second quarter of the twenty-first century. Again the OPEC countries of the Middle East and Latin America will continue to be major economic influences. On the other hand, the report considers that the European Community's share of world income will decline, and that all European countries will face difficult problems of structural adjustment. It is also suggested that the Soviet Union is likely to reach the peak of its power towards the end of the century.

(c) North/South: a Programme for Survival

Another general statement of world development needs was *North/South: A Programme for Survival* (1980), the Report of the Independent Commission on International Development Issues, under the chairmanship of Willy Brandt, with the support of a wide range of statesmen and other authorities from both the developing and developed world. It took its title from the belief that major new world-wide political initiatives are necessary if mankind is going to survive into the twenty-first century. It pointed out that hundreds of millions of people today live on the edge of starvation in the poorer, underdeveloped countries. The question was asked 'How can such countries ensure an economic environment in which they can cope with their own problems?' It suggests that the industrialised countries of the North have so far been unwilling to go very far towards accepting the South's case that the world's economy works to the South's disadvantage.

(d) Global 2000 Report to the US President

Recently, yet another report has been produced on world prospects to the end of the century. This is the *Global 2000 Report to the President*, 'Entering the twenty-first century: Volume I, a Summary report; Volume II, a Technical report; and Volume III, the Government's Global model'. It represents the first attempt by the US Government to produce an inter-related study of population, resource and environmental projections, providing the most consistent set of global projections yet achieved by US agencies. The study has three major underlying assumptions:

(i) a general continuation world-wide of present public policies relating to population stabilisation, natural resource conservation, and environmental protection;

(ii)   that rapid rates of technological development and adoption will con-
       tinue, with no serious social resistance, and that there will be no
       revolutionary changes or disastrous setbacks; and

(iii) no major disturbances of international trade as a result of war,
       political upheaval or a disturbance of the international monetary
       system.

The overall conclusion is that if present trends continue, by the year
2000 the world will be more crowded, more polluted, less stable
technologically, and more vulnerable to disruption. Barring revolutionary
advances in technology, life for most people on earth will be more
precarious than it is now, unless the nations of the world act decisively
to alter current trends. The report includes a number of findings, the
principal characteristics of which are as follows:

World population, by the year 2000, will have increased by more than
50 per cent, under medium growth projections, to something in the order
of 6.35 billion. The rate of growth will be slowing only marginally, from
1.8 per cent per year to 1.7 per cent. Population will be growing faster
by the end of the century than it is today, with 100 million people being
added every year compared to 75 million in 1975. Perhaps more
critically, 90 per cent of the population growth will be occurring in the
poorest countries. In terms of income, GNPs, which are recognised as
a rough and inadequate measure of social and economic welfare, will
increase by 53 per cent on a per capita basis, from $1,500 in 1975 to
$2,300 in the year 2000. However, present income disparities between
the rich and poor nations will probably have widened; for every $1
increase in GNP per capita in the less-developed countries, a $20 increase
is projected for the industrialised countries.

Food production will remain of critical importance. It is projected to
increase by 90 per cent over the period to the year 2000, a global per
capita increase of less than 15 per cent, but the bulk of this increase will
be in those countries which already have high food consumption. Real
prices for food are expected to double during the period. This projection relates to the availability of land. It is thought that arable land will
increase by only 4 per cent by the year 2000, so much of the increased
output will have to come from higher average yields. Most of the elements

that now contribute to high yields, such as fertilisers, pesticides, power for irrigation and fuel for machinery, depend heavily on oil and gas.

During the 1990s world *oil production* will be approaching maximum capacity. The richer nations will be able to command enough oil and other energy supplies to meet rising demands through the 1990s, but with the expected price increases many less-developed countries will have increasing difficulties in meeting their energy needs. The outlook is regarded as being especially bleak for the one-quarter of mankind which depends primarily upon wood for fuel.

Non-fuel minerals are considered sufficient to meet projected demands through to the end of the century, though production costs will increase with energy prices, making some mineral resources uneconomic. One-quarter of the world's population in the major industrialised and industrialising countries will continue to use three-quarters of the world's mineral production.

Water supplies are also thought likely to present particular problems in many areas. An increase of 200 to 300 per cent in world water usage is expected by the end of the century. The largest part of this will be for irrigation, which currently accounts for 70 per cent of human use of water. However, in many less-developed countries, water supplies will become erratic as a result of extensive de-forestation, and water pollution from heavy application of pesticides will cause difficulties. The use of pesticides in the less-developed countries is expected to increase by 4 to 6 times by the end of the century.

Linking into this is the role of *the forests*, where significant losses will continue as demand for wood products and fuel woods also increases. Growing stocks of commercial-size timber are expected to expand by 15 per cent per capita. Serious deterioration of agricultural soils will occur world-wide, with 'desertification', salinisation, alkalisation and water-logging. Moreover, in the atmosphere, concentrations of carbon dioxide and ozone-depleting chemicals are expected to increase at rates that could alter the world's climate and atmosphere significantly by 2050. There will be 'acid rain' from increased combustion of fossil fuels which will threaten lakes, soils and crops.

Finally, in terms of *species*, the extinction of plant and animal species will be increased dramatically; perhaps 20 per cent of all species on earth will be irretrievably lost as their habitats vanish, especially in the tropical forests.

While the Global 2000 report clearly has a pessimistic feel about it, the main purpose is to spell out the type of problems which an integrated approach is thought to throw up. For the US government the main need will remain a thorough assessment of its foreign and domestic policies relating to such key issues as population, resources and the environment. To meet the challenges described in the global study, it is emphasised that the US must improve its ability to identify emerging problems and assess alternative responses. The US government will also need a mechanism for continuous review of the assumptions used by the federal agencies for their projection models which supported the overall report.

1.7   Global Interdependence or Divergence

It will be apparent from the foregoing that many of the world's problems outlined in this chapter reflect a high degree of market interdependency which now extends across continents and cultures. Some observers feel that the growth of world-wide communications and the nature of the political, economic and social problems facing the international community will force even more interdependency in the future. This might be succinctly described as the 'one-world' view. In the business world the huge post-war growth of multinational companies and the integration and intensification of global markets and competition is here to stay. Yet other observers have also been impressed by the tendency of the world's political, economic and social forces to break into highly competitive or antagonistic groups in the future. This view has greater acceptance by those with a more nationalistic and regionally based view of the future for mankind. Whether convergency or divergency within the world community eventually triumphs remains to be seen. Certainly, whatever form future geo-political and economic power alignments take, the maintenance of peace and the avoidance of disastrous nuclear wars underly all hopes for mankind. Within this broad global scene the business planner must chart his own course. The essential management task and priority is, having taken a wide-ranging global view of the historical, political, economic, social and technological forces at work, then to devise effective company or organisational strategies and procedures to deal with the challenges and opportunities which present themselves. This is what the world of the international manager is now about.

A company's global strategic process must therefore include the following elements:

1. Making a situation audit of past, present and future in diverse markets.
2. Looking at threats and opportunities, strengths and weaknesses in these markets.
3. Defining purposes and missions on a truly international basis.
4. Seeking realistic goals and objectives for different markets and regions of the world.
5. Developing strategic options which are appropriate to diverse markets.
6. Implementing chosen strategies on a global basis.

2

The Role of The Multinational Enterprise

By way of introduction, the nature of global competition within the motor industry illustrates many of the issues facing international business today. In a supplement in the *Financial Times* on the motor industry (14 October 1986) four broad trends were suggested as being important, as the globally-based motor industry continues along the path of major and expensive market and technology changes.

(a) The financial recovery of the major European motor manufacturers in the 1980s was faster and stronger than most commentators or observers had previously dared to predict.

(b) The restructuring of the West European motor industry has been increasingly intensive because national governments are now much less willing to pay the high price of subsidies to protect the motor industry jobs.

(c) The USA which, not so long ago, provided 30 per cent of local car sales and 50 per cent of profits, is no longer the 'honey pot' it once was, following the steady fall in the value of the US dollar.
      This rapidly changing market situation is having a major impact on those European producers, like BMW, Porsche and Jaguar, who have been exporting high-price, luxury cars to the USA, and also on the volume-producing Japanese car companies, who have been exporting over one million cars a year to the USA.

(d) Meanwhile, the three big US global manufacturers — General Motors, Ford and Chrysler — have taken strategic decisions to supply many of their components for small cars from lower-cost suppliers in the Far East, i.e. South Korea and Taiwan. These newly-industrialised countries have become increasingly important in the industry because of the support they are getting from the major American car manufactuers. In the 1970s the financial state of much of the European motor industry was a real cause for concern. However, by the mid-1980s manufacturers had cut their costs dramatically in the face of extreme competition, and for some companies at least this policy was beginning to pay significant dividends in terms of reduction of costs and improved profitability.

The global reality is that the world's motor industry of today can no longer be regarded as something concerned with local or national markets. Any discusson of the motor industry inevitably involves an analysis of *world issues*, including competition, investment, manufacture and financial strategies. The internationalisation of the motor business is reflected in many other related industries, including steel, rubber, plastics, glass and electrical components, etc. Similar developments are also apparent in most other manufacturing and service industries which operate globally.

2.1   The Evolution of International Markets

John Dunning, in Chapter 5 of *The Growth of International Business* (Casson, ed., 1983), traced the evolution of the modern multinational enterprise from two broad categories of multinational enterprises that developed in the last century. On the one hand there were *supply-orientated* multinational enterprises, which were mainly concerned with primary products, though in some cases they later developed as vertically-integrated manufacturing companies. The primary sectors covered such products as oil, copper, precious metals, and food stuffs, transforming them into more sophisticated products, and including substantial secondary processing with an eventual integration into consumer markets in many different parts of the world. In recent times the decline in the supply-orientated international production in less-developed countries has been due to the improvement in the commodity markets, and also because of the risk of ex-appropriation through nationalisation. Nevertheless, many of the modern multinationals do trace their roots back to companies that were originally concerned with the development of the production and distribution of basic raw materials.

Another line of development was from *market-orientated* multi-nationals, many of which developed out of the great trading companies of the nineteenth century. These, in turn, moved forward to a variety of developments by integrating production on a world-wide basis and by gradually introducing advanced technologies, by spreading out geographically and by diversifying.

The development of the modern multinationals must also be seen within the growth of the international economy as a whole, and the many changes which have impacted on it. For instance, the post-war era also saw the reconstruction and growth of the Western European and Japanese economies which, in their turn, have extended multinational activities to many other parts of the world.

Another development of great importance during the past two decades has been the emergence of the newly-industrialising countries, most of which have owed a great deal to the technology and the investment introduced into them by modern multinational companies, who have often been in search of both new sources of labour and new export possibilities. The foot-loose nature of multinational investment today, the ability of huge companies to re-deploy assets and technology on a global basis to create new manufacturing capacity and to develop global markets, has become one of the most important characteristics of the contemporary international scene. This, in turn, has sometimes brought them into acute conflicts with many national governments concerned with the maintenance of sovereign powers over their domestic economies. In many developing countries political independence has gone hand-in-hand with processes leading to the extension of multinational ownership and extension of control into many facets of the increasingly globally interdependent economy.

2.2   Defining the Multinational Company

It will be apparent from the foregoing that the term 'multinational company' applies to a variety of definitions extending from a company with production located in two or more countries, to a more restrictive definition of a management philosophy which is 'outward-looking' with international awareness. Understanding of the term has been further complicated by additional descriptions from trans-national (used by the United Nations) to the more loosely called 'international company', which may have a large part of its earnings from exports or related activities.

The permanency of the multinational, when a group of companies form a consortium or syndicate for a particular period of time, limited to purposes or one-off contracts (such as oil exploration or construction), adds definition problems in some cases. An arbitrary level of criteria used for defining *multinational* has been used for various levels of overseas asset locations, sales and the percentage of profits earned overseas.

The OECD in its *Guidelines for Multinational Enterprises* (1977) does not give a rigid definition but broadly describes present-day multinationals as:

> companies or entities whose ownership is private, state or mixed, established in different countries and so linked that one or more of them may be able to exercise a significant influence over the activities of others and, in particular, to share knowledge and resources with others.

The degree of autonomy of each entity in relation to the others varies widely from one multinational enterprise to another, depending on the nature of the links between such entities and the fields of activities concerned.

Thus, although activities may be located in more than one country, no minimum level is stipulated, neither is the type of activity. Companies engaged in manufacturing and mining would probably be considered by most as being multinational though few would regard national airlines with facilities located in different countries as multinational, but under the OECD definition they could be. Borderline cases are when food processors (such as Dalgety or Tate and Lyle) who are engaged in a manufacturing process are also largely involved in trading of raw commodities and so could be considered as merely commodity trading houses. An awkward delineation between levels of processing would be necessary. The OECD definition also fails to describe the degree of control. Many commentators would agree that for a controlling influence, foreign direct investment should first be necessary before a company could be classified as multinational, rather than just a domestic company with many overseas portfolio investments. Usually, to guarantee control of a company, over 50 per cent of the voting equity should be held by the parent multinational. Often though, effective control can be exercised with a much smaller holding, but in contrast, where government restrictions are imposed, even a 50 per cent-plus equity holding may not be sufficient. The British Government's £1 special share in Britoil and its limitations on Enterprise Oil when it too was privatised are examples.

Control, however, can be highly effective even without equity control when licensing or franchises are undertaken. Royalty payments can be seen as overseas-derived income just as consolidated sales in the company's annual accounts. Companies like Heublein who owned the Kentucky Fried Chicken franchise and Coca Cola could be considered as multinational with their world-wide activities, yet most of their income comes from franchise fees or technical royalties and not from direct sales. The modern definition of MNEs has therefore had numerous interpretations.

Just as there are great variations in the *definitions* of what constitutes a multinational, so there are many differing theories about the *existence* and *growth* of multinationals. Buckley and Casson in *The Economic Theory of the Multinational Enterprise* (1985) suggest that no single theory is adequate and even the widely-accepted transactions cost explanation of MNE growth is deficient. No single theory is able to explain why some MNEs enter certain markets or why different forms of enterprise are undertaken. Dunning and others have also argued that MNEs will begin overseas operations if they have location advantages (i.e. it is cheaper than exporting) or ownership advantages (i.e. that there are benefits from internalising costs such as transfer pricing to save tax). The first type can be examined under theories of capital movements, trade or location. The second type are covered by theories of industrial organisation, innovation, the firm and markets.

Historically, many economists have explained MNEs' foreign direct investment in terms of their location, usually in a colonial context and resource-based. However, following the large-scale post-World War II American investment in Europe, theories switched from country factors to company-specific factors such as ownership and internalisation.

2.3 Major Multinational Companies in the 1980s

As shown previously, the problems of definition of a multinational company and the numerous different meanings used by various studies make comparisons difficult.

A regular and fairly consistent grouping over time are the annual *Fortune 500* and *Foreign 500* company listings. In 1983 on those lists, which cover only industrial companies which are either state-owned or quoted corporations, there were 295 US-based companies and 428 non-US, each with a turnover of over one billion dollars. For non-US companies, dollar revenues are calculated by the use of average exchange rates rather than end-year rates which could be more susceptible to short-term fluctuations.

Of the 1983 total, 44 companies were subsidiaries of other companies already included in the number, for example, Sohio (majority owned by BP), Ford Motor UK (owned by Ford USA). Of the remaining 679, probably under 30 can be considered, under the criterion of manufacturing located in six countries, not to be multinational. Of the 679 companies, 284 were based in the United States, 69 in the United Kingdom, 44 in West Germany, 31 in France and 115 in Japan.

A study conducted in 1977 by the United Nations of 10,727 companies with foreign direct investments showed a similar pattern of location of parent companies (Table 2.1).

Table 2.1

Country	Number of companies	Country	Number of companies
United States	2,826	France	599
Britain	1,706	Canada	452
W. Germany	1,450	Japan	382
Switzerland	871	Others	1,819
Holland	622		

The study also noted that all of these countries, except for Japan, had more of their subsidiaries located in other developed countries than located in developing countries.

Looking at the 679 billion-dollar revenue companies of 1983, the pattern of industrial distribution is seen in Table 2.2. The high technology industries dominate along with chemicals and pharmaceuticals. However, the more basic industrials in foods and oil are the next most prominent groups.

An analysis of the billion-dollar companies in 1983 by country of origin is given in Table 2.3. As in most cases, if most of a company's revenue is earned in its home country then currency effects can distort the relative size of companies.

A further and possibly better measure for comparison of company sizes is market capitalisation. This is the market value of the company's shares

Table 2.2

	Number of companies		Number of companies
Oil	84	Industrial and Transport	
Metal Manufacturing	82	Equipment	41
Food, Drink, Tobacco	94	Wood, Paper, Publishing	49
Electronics, Telecoms,		Building Materials	26
Aerospace	113	Mining	16
Chemicals,		Textiles and Clothing	17
Pharmaceuticals,		Rubber	14
Cosmetics	96	Shipbuilding	10
Motor Vehicles and			
Parts	37	Total	679

NOTE: Conglomerates, where appropriate, have been included under their principal group industry.

Table 2.3

Country	Number of companies	Total revenues $ bn	Country	Number of companies	Total revenues $ bn
United States	285	1,507	Brazil	2	18
Japan	115	375	Mexico	2	17
Britain	69	246	Austria	2	9
W. Germany	44	203	Taiwan	2	8
France	31	142	Norway	2	8
Canada	23	57	Chile	2	3
Sweden	17	33	Kuwait	1	11
Switzerland	11	47	Argentina	1	7
Korea	10	48	Venezuela	1	6
Italy	9	80	Netherlands/		
Holland	8	115	Antilles	1	6
S. Africa	8	17	Israel	1	3
Australia	7	14	Portugal	1	2
Spain	6	25	Philippines	1	2
Belgium	4	18	Colombia	1	2
Finland	4	8	New Zealand	1	2
India	3	14	Zambia	1	2
Turkey	3	9	Peru	1	1
			Total	679	3,062

multiplied by the number of shares issued. Comparisons of capitalisation are more volatile on a daily basis as share prices vary frequently and, therefore, so does the market capitalisation. However, comparisons can be made for any day and not just on year-end or quarterly accounts. Capitalisation reflects the asset size (partially by issued capital) and performance (implicit in the price of the shares, which varies with earnings and asset backing). For non-freely traded shares, asset size or revenue comparisons may be the only way to compare company size (though even these may not be available from privately held companies).

Capital International in a private survey showed 257 companies worldwide with a capitalisation over $2 billion; their domestic headquarters were located as shown in Table 2.4.

Table 2.4

United States	155	South Africa	3
Japan	45	Holland	3
Britain	18	Australia	2
Canada	12	Italy	1
W. Germany	10	Singapore	1
Switzerland	6	Hong Kong	1

These companies in October 1983, however, include some duplication, e.g. Unilever NV and Unilever Plc, as well as service industries, stores, banks, etc. Comparing market capitalisation, though, has an advantage in that some, albeit inadequate, comparison of company size can be made between widely varying commercial activities such as with banks which have no measurable turnover.

2.4 World Business as Foreign Direct Investment

In 1982 this amounted to some 550 billion dollars. The location of foreign investment has been noted by two major surveys, one by the United Nations, the other by the US Department of Commerce. The UN survey showed that by value, eight developed market economies in 1978 accounted for over 93 per cent of the origin or supply of total world foreign direct investment. The US data showed (Table 2.5) that since 1960 the proportion of world foreign direct investment by British companies

Table 2.5 Sources of World Stock of Foreign Direct Investment ($ billion)

	1960	1967	1973	1978	1981
United States	31.9	56.6	101.3	162.7	226.4
United Kingdom	10.8	17.5	26.9	41.1	65.5
Others	23.1	41.0	84.9	175.1	253.7
Total	65.8	115.1	213.1	378.9	545.6

Source: US Department of Commerce

had fallen from over 16 per cent to 12 per cent in 1981. The United States investment share fell by 7 per cent to 41 per cent during the period. However, in the two decades between 1960 and 1981 total foreign direct investment had risen over 700 per cent (around 170 per cent in real terms, after allowing for US consumer inflation).

Of the remaining 35 per cent ($23 billion) of foreign direct investment in 1960, 10.6 per cent was from Holland, 6.2 per cent from France, 1.2 per cent from West Germany, 0.8 per cent from Japan, and only 1.1 per cent from developing countries. By 1981, West Germany had 8.3 per cent of world foreign direct investment, Japan 6.8 per cent, Holland only 5.9 per cent, France fell to 4.5 per cent, and the developing countries' share rose to 3.2 per cent. Thus, despite relative declines by older investors, other developed, mainly Western European countries have increased their overseas presence. Developing countries have had little growth in their foreign direct investment except for the OPEC countries which, during the 1970s, built up reserves of petro-dollars and overseas investments, though often rather as portfolio investments as seen by the Kuwait Investment Office.

Though data on foreign investment is generally scarce, information on American investment has been more consistently collated and IMF figures on balance of payments data, including investment flows, have provided an overall picture of foreign direct investment developments. The predominant size of American investment can thus be briefly examined with reference to its stock, location and resulting income flows.

American foreign direct investment rose from under $12 billion in 1950 to $25 billion in 1957 and over $220 billion in 1982. In the early 1950s a third was invested in Canada but by the early 1980s this had fallen to a fifth. American investment in Britain rose from over 7 per cent of the total in 1950 to 14 per cent in 1982. Total American investment in

Europe rose from $1.7 billion in 1950 to $99.9 billion in 1982 (14.7 per cent to 45.1 per cent). Investment in Japan rose rapidly from $19 million in 1950 to $6.8 billion in 1982 but still only represented 0.2 per cent and 3.1 per cent respectively of total US foreign direct investment. Investment by Americans in less-developed countries fell relatively from 48.7 per cent in 1950 to 24.0 per cent in 1982. Latin America did worst with the debt problems reducing confidence in their economies. Investment in them fell from 38.8 per cent of total to 14.9 per cent though by value it rose by $28.5 billion to $33 billion.

Investment in Brazil rose strongly between the mid-1960s and mid-1970s after slow growth during the 1950s. Since 1977 the growth of American foreign direct investment in Brazil has kept pace with the average growth rate. In Mexico the pattern of investment has been broadly similar with slower than average growth between 1950—66, and faster growth since 1977. However, in 1982 the stock of American foreign direct investment in Mexico fell from $7 billion in 1981 to $5.6 billion, primarily due to a decline in the value of the peso.

The US stock of investment in Taiwan, Korea and Singapore soared from virtually nil in the 1950s to under $100 million in 1966 to $3.2 billion in 1982, over half of which was located in Singapore (aptly known as the multinational state).

The results of these US foreign direct investments have been outflows of dividends, royalties and other financial transfers from the newly industrialised countries (NICs) and other countries to America.

In 1950 the total annual income from foreign direct investment in Brazil was yielding 15 per cent at almost $100 million. In Mexico the yield was 10 per cent at $43 million. By 1966 the investment stock of $1.3 billion in Mexico was yielding $108 million, around 8 per cent. In Brazil the yield was 12 per cent on $0.9 billion. Americans had surprisingly invested more heavily in the lower return country, Mexico. Although the speed of income flows could be different and thus explain the relatively lower profitability of Mexico compared with Brazil, the yield for Mexico in 1981 was $1.4 billion on $7 billion, a 19 per cent return, but in 1982 it was negative with the $1.3 billion fall in capital values giving minus 18 per cent. Brazil in 1981 yielded 6 per cent and in 1982 10 per cent, illustrating the apparently poor choice of Mexico for the stock of $7 billion of investment in 1981. Mexico, however, has undoubtedly benefited financially from this capital inflow as has Brazil, though the dividends, royalties and other fees paid by Brazil have been expensive at an annual average of $600 million over the debt-burden period 1978—82.

The three Far East newly industrialised countries (Taiwan, Korea and Singapore) have yielded a total of $2.5 billion over the six years to 1982, on an average of $2.2 billion, an annual yield of 25 per cent for Singapore, 7 per cent for Korea and 18 per cent for Taiwan. The average return for all locations of American foreign direct investment for 1977—82 was 15 per cent. The highest yielding area, paradoxically, is the one to which the least new investment was allocated: the less-developed countries which earned a 23 per cent annual average return between 1977—82. The explanation is probably that the higher risks involved in investing in a developing country require higher rewards. The NICs have been more highly regarded and thus 'lower' returns accepted. The Latins' geographic proximity has probably been a further consideration for 'reduced risk'. Singapore, however, would not appear to have been in the 'highest risk' category, but its rapid economic growth (almost the highest in the world between 1960—82) has facilitated above-average returns.

2.5   Global Reach and the Nation State

Many academic and other commentators have given considerable attention to the problem of relating the interests of multinational companies to different national situations and contexts. At the industrial and commercial level, there has been pressure on multinationals endlessly to extend and widen their global markets. This has meant that manufacturing and service companies originally based in the USA, Western Europe, Japan and the newly industrialising countries, have found it imperative, for a host of technical and commercial reasons, to establish wider operations and activities. The search for global economies has become a paramount need.

The post-World War II era also saw the end of the colonial empires and the emergence of well over a hundred new sovereign countries, all of which have been anxious to establish for themselves a sense of legitimacy and autonomy. Many of these countries have felt greatly threatened by the global extent of multinational activities. Political independence has come at the same time as an intensification of the growth of global commercial interdependence. It has proved to be an uneasy partnership. The sense of unease and conflict has not been confined to the developing countries. Indeed, one of the most important reactions against modern multinational activities was first expressed in Western Europe in the 1950s and 60s, when the global impact and scale of American multinational enterprise was first experienced. Later, in the 1970s, much commentary came from the United Nations Commission on Transnational Corporations, which has reflected on the desirability or otherwise of these global activities and trends.

Richard Robinson, in his book *International Business Management* (1978), points out:

> The geographically defined nation state is a product of a unique geopolitical position, a unique historical input, a unique ethnic mix and a unique democratic record. For a state so defined to survive more than a fleeting historical moment, it must enjoy the loyalty of most of its residents. Some would call this personal identification or loyalty nationalism, others patriotism.

Whatever is followed, countries and companies establish their own national priorities, which may or may not coincide much of the time. They certainly give priority to resource allocation in many different ways. Robinson lists these choices as follows:

(a) To invest in the wherewithal of future production and consumption or of present production and consumption;

(b) To a military establishment or to the civilian sector;

(c) To the private market sector or to the public sector;

(d) To human resource development or to the development of physical assets;

(e) To the achievement of full employment or to achievement of technical efficiency;

(f) To the achievement of international integration or to national autarchy;

(g) To the achievement of maximum efficiency of resource use or of decentralisation of economic power by forced competition;

(h) To the achievement of maximum efficiency or of a more even level of development (that is, from one part of the country to another);

(i) To a reward system based on the market value of one's product (*laissez-faire*) or to the assurance of a given level of consumption to all (that is, welfare);

(j) To the preservation of environmental integrity or to the unrestrained exploitation of the environment.

Another important perception Robinson brings to looking at the international system, is what he calls *variables*. He lists these under a number of headings:

(i) different national sovereignties,
(ii) disparate national economic conditions,
(iii) different national values and institutions,
(iv) difference in timing of national industrial revolution,
(v) geographical distance,
(vi) different areas of population, etc.

All of these lead to a development of different responses, and differences of national policies and power, which require multinational companies to respond in various ways. Indeed, an important part of the challenge for the multinational manager is to analyse accurately the nature of the local political, social, economic and historical environment, and then link his own company strategies and policies into an effective relationship.

2.6 Britain and the Multinationals

Chapter 1 outlined Britain's changing geo-political role within the expanding European Community. Britain remains the world's second largest multinational investor after the United States, and is also probably the second most popular investment site for multinational companies to establish new activities. In the immediate post-war years, the main source of multinational investment was from the USA, and the 1950s brought an immense increase of activities of all sorts. At that time J.H. Dunning wrote an important book on *American Investment in British Manufacturing Industry* (Dunning 1958). Later in the 1960s increasing public concern was felt about the implications for British industry of heavy investment overseas and research was undertaken by W.D. Reddaway, in collaboration with others, on *Effects of UK Investment Overseas* (Reddaway 1968). In general, the view was that such overseas investment was beneficial to British exports, and therefore in the longer run was also beneficial to employment within the British economy as a whole.

The 1970s and 80s, characterised as they were by a tremendous increase in global competition, also witnessed a drastic reduction in the *relative competitiveness* of many famous British companies. There was a serious loss of traditional markets overseas, and at the same time a massive increase in the scale of import penetration into hitherto secure home markets. Increasingly, British consumers became accustomed to buying a wide range of consumer and other products from overseas and indeed in many cases abandoned brand loyalty to traditional British products. At the same time labour productivity in many companies increased and total outputs rose. One result of these trends was a huge decline in the numbers employed in manufacture within the British Isles, the workforce falling from something over 10 million in the early 1970s, to 5 million today. The more than halving of the workforce in manufacturing activities became a continuing contentious element in the political economy of Britain during the last two decades. Increases in manufacturing efficiency and productivity have gone hand-in-hand with a dramatic decline in the size of the home workforce. At the same time, the loss of markets, both domestic and overseas, has made it difficult for many British companies, especially in consumer goods, to maintain their previous market positions at home and abroad.

A recent serious analytical study, *Britain and the Multinationals* (Stopford and Turner 1985), looks at both the performance of British multinationals, and also foreign direct investment in the UK. The central theme is that during the past two decades British companies could no longer base their activities on developing purely national market strategies, or treat their foreign operations as peripheral. Rather the global economy, they argue, has now become crucial to industrial strategies, because competition has become global. The growth of this world-wide competition has intensified due to the fact that the world's major industries have often become dominated by a few giant firms. To compete against such global giants firms are forced to think globally themselves. For British companies the national market of the United Kingdom is inadequate to create the economies of scale, or to pay for the huge 'start up' sums needed for technological innovation. Yet such factors are vital to hold on to world leadership in such industries as automobiles, computers or electronics. Global competition is also a result of the globalisation of taste which has gone on in many markets.

Amongst other key national industrial strategy questions raised by the Stopford and Turner book are:

(a) A widespread belief that as many British-owned multinationals have been shifting production, trade and services to overseas locations, this has done fundamental harm to the home economy. The authors offer no clear-cut answers. However, they do point out, as Reddaway did before them, that the existence of many British firms operating abroad does in fact often create British exports, which can maintain, or indeed increase some employment, at least for a time.

(b) Perhaps more importantly — are British multinationals today in the right industrial sectors to ensure continuing high status and prestige and effectiveness to the British economy as a whole? Britain still has a leadership position in many industries such as food, drink, tobacco and other low technology trades. However, she is often under-represented in high technology areas, other than the *defence industry*, which have a predominant role in the economy as a whole.

To some extent, this under-representation in high technology manufacture is compensated for by the strong position held in multinational activities by British service industries, notably the banking and insurance sectors. It was also assisted by the strong earnings from North Sea oil.

(c) Has Britain's predominantly *laissez-faire* policy towards trade and investment now come to a time for revision, especially since foreign firms set up low-wage and low-skill plants here, while British multinationals, often in higher technology industries, are themselves moving abroad?

The question arises as to what would happen in the absence of such foreign investment in the British economy throughout the 1970s into the 1990s. A general view is that the present scale of global competition means that Britain has little alternative but to remain an *open economy*, competing for investment funds and markets on a global market basis. This has important implications for British politics. If, for example, a left-wing government restricted outward investment or forced the repatriation of such homeward, this might in fact lead to other policies abroad which would be counter-productive for Britain's survival in global markets. Indeed, it is suggested that UK companies must be permitted to continue to compete in overseas markets and to invest and set up plants overseas. Unless one is thinking of creating a totally autarchical closed economy, any policy restricting overseas investment, either inwards or outwards, harms companies' competitiveness in the domestic economy.

(d) A fourth point involves the role of the state. The position is that today industry has become so globalised that there remain few unilateral decisions which are in fact open to a radical UK government, when confronted with the facts of international investment flows. Given the presence of so many multinationals in countries like the USA, which are the home base of so many multinationals in Britain, any policy attempting to control such companies in the

UK would speedily invite retaliation by the USA. The internationalisation of business challenges the power of the nation in all parts of the world. Britain is not exempt from this global competitive situation.

One possible means of restoring the position *vis-à-vis* the multinationals might be for the UK government to co-operate with similar minded governments in Europe in devising a common policy or strategy towards foreign multinationals. As yet there have been only limited signs that this is a feasible policy. The diverse interests of the European nation states, both within and beyond the European Community, have made it difficult for them to develop common policies towards multinational activities whether they derive from each other, or from the USA or, more recently, from Japan and other countries in the Far East. The political implications of this global competition are of crucial importance to the sovereign power and standing of the European nation states, both within and outside the European Community.

2.7 The Organisation of Global Business

Many authors have developed elaborate theories about the way in which companies develop markets overseas and subsequently modify their organisation and behaviour to suit new circumstances. Figure 2.1 shows how, following on from the decision to sell abroad, companies may go into exporting by direct or indirect means. They may then move through to licensing arrangements and on to the establishment of overseas marketing branches or subsidiaries. At a later stage the decision to produce abroad leads to the establishment of a wholly owned plant or, more commonly, a plant owned in joint venture with an overseas partner. Moving through these stages causes companies to go through various organisational and cultural identity changes. The more global a company becomes, the more its own internal culture has to establish new responses to the changing situations in which it finds itself.

Some commentators have given particular attention to what happens to the management and decision making systems of companies once they become involved with more products in more countries. Michael Z. Brooke in his *International Management* (Brooke 1987) points to the problems and conflicts of decision-making processes when they are transposed to a number of different, globally extending organisational structures. He suggests that in a multinational company all of these structures

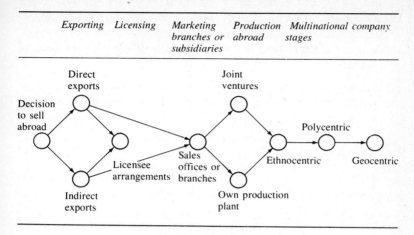

Exporting	Licensing	Marketing branches or subsidiaries	Production abroad	Multinational company stages

STAGES OF FOREIGN INVOLVEMENT BY COMPANIES

Stage	Nature of activity	Management skills and attitude/ Corporate organisation
One	Exports–Imports	Minimum change in home country operations
Two	Foreign licensing and international movement of 'know-how'	Small change but still little impact on home country operations
Three	Establishment of overseas operations, i.e. substantial investment in funds and management time	Develops special international skills but with separate home country and international organisation
Four	Emergence as a world enterprise	Increased global approach and organisation

Figure 2.1   The Development of an International Market

are likely to be unstable and subject to change and variation. He considers that they can be sorted into the following main types, according to the principal responsibility for the foreign operation:

(a) *Functional activities.* Head office management devises global policies, and the foreign subsidiary reports to managers with overall, company-wide responsibilities.

(b) *Geographical*. The management of the foreign operations is delegated to a special unit which may be called an international division, or into several units each with responsibility for a region or country.

(c) *Product group*. The foreign subsidiaries are managed directly by the product divisions at home which take their own decisions about foreign markets.

(d) *Matrix*. Geographical and product divisions are jointly responsible for the foreign operations.

(e) *Project. Ad hoc* groups are appointed to manage the foreign operations at different stages in their development.

In the final analysis managerial responsibility generally means responsibility for profit, and accountability as well as authority in exercising control. The implication of all this is that the organisational structure adopted by multinational companies influences the way the accounts are made up, and how successful and unsuccessful units are identified on a global basis.

2.8   World Finance and 'Big Bang'

Any discussions about international business today would be incomplete without reference to the rapidly changing circumstances and functioning of global financial dealings centred on New York, London, Tokyo, Singapore, Hong Kong and elsewhere. As outlined in Chapter 1 America's huge post-war surpluses were used to finance the reconstruction of Europe through the Marshall Plan and also supported massive world-wide investments by US multinational companies, which created new industries in Western Europe, Australasia and the Far East, and in Africa and Latin America. Successive GATT negotiations led to greatly liberalised trade on a world basis. Between the 1950s and 1970s trade grew at 8 per cent per annum, significantly faster than world output. The newly industrialising countries emerged as exporters of manufactures, while buoyant commodity prices also encouraged development.

In the 1970s new problems emerged. Inflationary pressures both stimulated and later came from the OPEC oil price rises of the 1970s. Oil prices have fluctuated widely in the 1980s. Global industrial output also fluctuated, while most primary producers experienced significant deterioration in their terms of trade. Investment capital, abundant from the OPEC oil surpluses of the 1970s, had led to over-borrowing by many Eastern European and developing countries, and brought major debt difficulties which were intensified by the 1980—82 recession in the industrial countries. The move to high interest rates in the USA and elsewhere in the early 1980s, which gave investors a significant real rate of return over inflation, for the first time in two decades, also imposed acute pressures on borrowers confronted with sluggish markets and low earnings or even losses on many of their newly acquired assets.

During the 1980s, the so-called 'locomotive of the Western industrial system' — the American economy — grew strongly, but at the cost of both a sharp diminution in domestic savings and a rise in both the US Government's deficit and a huge increase in the nation's current account deficit. Japan, with a high savings ratio, became a major investor in US Government loan stocks. By the end of 1986 America's current account deficit had reached $126.7 billion, a value of about 34 per cent of the USA's total exports of goods and services, or 3 per cent of GNP, despite the maintenance of high interest rates and the sharp depreciation of the dollar since 1985. Meanwhile, America's widening external deficit was mirrored by surpluses in the other industrial countries, notably West Germany with $44.3 billion and Japan with $87.5 billion in 1986. There were strong calls for protectionism in American industry, though the Uruguay round of multilateral trade negotiations between major industrial countries in 1986 did produce a commitment to maintain free world trade.

Paralleling these many developments in the nature of the world's financial markets has been the intensified globalisation of competition between the world's money markets. In the 1950s and 1960s American banks increasingly moved around the world, closely associated with the extension of American multinational companies into new markets. The 1960s brought the growth of the Euro-dollar market, which meant that many companies increasingly financed themselves from off-shore dollar funds which were not repatriated to the USA. In the 1970s a vast increase in OPEC oil surpluses also provided an entirely new source of dollar-denominated funds for 'recycling' and redeployment by Western banks on a global basis. The move of the USA away from a fixed relationship of the dollar with gold and the introduction of, at first flexible, and then floating exchange rates for the world's major trading currencies further transformed the hitherto structured basis for international finance and trade. In order to survive, national banks had to seek international markets, and look for a future on a global basis.

Similar developments led to greater freedom in other financial markets as well, and the major world financial centres of London, New York, Singapore, Hong Kong and Tokyo were increasingly seen as operating in and competing for the same business. The introduction of electronic means of communication for all types of financial and other transactions accelerated the changes. In London, in the mid-1980s, wholesale changes in the structure and regulation of financial markets, including an abandonment of the traditional distinction between jobbers and brokers in the Stock Exchange, and the take-over of many hitherto independent stockbroking firms by larger financial groups — popularly known as 'Big Bang' — indicate the scale of the transformations. For a long period of post-war history, the maintenance of the sterling area and of *fixed rates of exchange* for the dollar and sterling was seen as an essential element in the British political and economic scene. Paradoxically, the abandonment of this system led to London enjoying enormous prosperity, as overseas banks and other institutions poured in to capitalise on Britain's unrivalled position as a global financial centre, freely trading in all types of convertible currencies and other financial instruments. The freeing of both national and international markets and the competition which now clearly exists between the world's leading financial centres, linked as they are by electronic trading, indicates the extent to which globalisation has gone. There is no reason to assume that these developments are at an end. The global linkage of financial markets means that the ups and downs, the confidence and activities in one part of the world, can in a flash be translated to other markets!

Of particular structural importance is the continuing financial plight of many of the developing countries. Over-borrowing by the less developed countries has been given much prominence in the financial press. Broadly, up until the early 1980s there was a strong inflow of both public and private lending to the developing countries. Most of these inflows came through the American and European banks, and were based on the very large cash deposits built up by OPEC states. In 1981 net flows to developing countries were $75.7 billion and in 1982 $68.9 billion. By 1986 they had collapsed to some $25.6 billion. In the meantime, the total debt outstanding to the developing countries rose from $49.8 billion in 1981 to $753.4 billion in 1986, and the average ratio of debt to GNP rose from just over one fifth to over one third. In most developing countries continuous debt restructuring became the order of the day, reflecting the weakening of their earning abilities from both traditional primary exports and also, in some cases, from oil. According to the World Bank, the 'central issue' for the highly indebted middle income countries is their need to finance new investments. The commercial banks have agreed to new approaches, including complex schemes of selling developing country debts at a discount and for converting such debts into equity. Chile and Mexico have employed this approach, and Nigeria and Argentina are considering similar plans. However, for the poorer countries of sub-Saharan Africa enormous problems of long-term financial needs still exist, which can only be met by concessional loan arrangements.

Finally, some measure of the scale of the current international debt problem can be gained from the fact that something like two-thirds of the total international debt outstanding in the developing countries involves borrowing by private companies or individuals without the support of government guarantees. However, the position of official creditors is often little better. In fact, in 1986 twenty-four countries renegotiated their debts with official creditors or commercial banks in various multinational fora. Again, in the same year, eighteen countries renegotiated debts with official creditors mainly through the 'Paris Club', which brings together representatives of the major central banks and lending agencies. In the longer term, the only solution to these truly global financial problems will be by structural adjustments which enable countries to operate in a financially viable way. The World Bank, in its 1987 *World Development Report*, also pointed to the need to identify investment priorities and to undertake only projects with high rates of return. However, it also emphasised the importance of the macro-economic environment — as it is virtually impossible to have a good project in a bad policy environment.

3

Strategic Thinking for International Markets

Chapters 1 and 2 have indicated the global viewpoints essential to the practising manager in devising effective international business strategies for the world of today. Clearly the growth of air travel and communications technology has created a degree of interdependency and global awareness inconceivable even a decade or so ago. Diplomats and soldiers have traditionally thought in terms of political and military power balances and of defending national interests and security. Business and industrial managers must now also learn to monitor and respond constantly to world events in terms of the security of their businesses. They must strategically evaluate rapidly changing global business risks and opportunities for the short, medium and longer term. Decisions must be made about what products their company is to export, when and where to appoint agents, to enter into joint ventures, or to make major investments in countries other than their own. Managers must also decide which international products and markets to concentrate on, and which to let go. The choice of *key markets* and products for intensive development, as opposed to those of more marginal concern, presents some of the most difficult management decisions in strategic forward planning for rapidly changing global markets.

3.1 Managers' Departure Points

It is essential for international managers to think widely about the world and about the opportunities and risks open to them and their businesses. In doing this, they will be influenced by many viewpoints. Of primary importance will be their own personal backgrounds.

(a) Many experienced international managers instinctively adopt an *inductive* scanning approach, looking at events historically and at the way that procedures and institutions have evolved over time. Taking a wide global viewpoint requires the manager to rely substantially on his own, or other people's, concrete experience of events and conditions, frequently based on the past situation — or, alternatively, by reflective observation of contemporary evidence as daily reported through the television and radio, the newspapers, or by the experience of travel. Such a broad, inductive view of the world has much to be said for it, in that it can assist the international manager in establishing a comprehensive *lateral thinking* viewpoint of the global market opportunities and risks facing his company.

(b) A second individual point of departure might be taken by focusing on a *deductive* scientific line of thought. This will be pursued by international managers who have had a scientific or mathematical training, and are looking for strong predictive certainties. Again, it generally takes two forms. It may involve them in active experimentation by setting up situations, carefully monitoring results, and drawing conclusions. On the other hand, the deductive thinker is also attracted to abstract concepts and theories, for which he then seeks to find examples to support particular practices or policies. A deductive approach has the merits of scientific rigour, though when it encounters diverse country and cultural market circumstances much time may be spent in seeking to establish quantitative certainties which in reality may be impossible to find.

(c) A third approach, probably most essential for the successful international manager, is to seek to take an *integrative* viewpoint, using the best of both the broad-scanning, historical and institutional view of the world, and combining it together with some of the analytical tools of the deductive, scientific and prediction-seeking approach, for devising sound strategies for the future. Integrated team-based management planning on the part of an international manager becomes a way of mixing together various ways of thinking into a decision-making system which can effectively encompass the complexity of rapidly changing and diverse global markets. The manager must blend together, in a meaningful way, the combined experience of the past with the many opportunities which undoubtedly lie in the future.

So much, then, for the different approaches which may be followed by international company managers seeking to take a view of the rapidly changing world and to plan effective company business and market strategies. In looking outward at global markets as a whole, their views of future opportunities and *risks* will be powerfully shaped by the ideas or paradigms of a number of diverse disciplines. The use of a *planning team* of company managers with diverse disciplinary backgrounds and experience in global markets is an essential approach to the complex thinking involved.

3.2   Political, Economic and Social Ideas

In looking at global markets, underlying economic and political circumstances are of critical importance. The economist faces the reality of *scarcity*. The world is analysed in terms of the relative finiteness of the environment and of basic resources, such as minerals, and by the shortness of human life. Scarcity is a fact of nature, which ultimately determines the relative availabilities and, therefore, the underlying costs and prices of all types of goods and services. The innovative international manager does not intend to be confined to allocating scarcity. He is in business to overcome this. His prime purpose is the organising and creation of new *wealth* in the form of goods and services, which in national economic terms are measured by Gross National Product (GNP). The consumer is thought of as desiring increases in his material consumption, both now and in the foreseeable future. In order to increase material consumption in both individual consumer and national wealth terms, positive strategies and actions are necessary. These strategies and actions link the desire for immediate consumption with, at the same time, a need to forego consumption and put aside savings for investment in order to create the wherewithal by which further wealth may be created for the future. A related way of viewing the world is afforded by the ideas of *welfare* and equity. As material wealth has increased, there are hopes by many for a more equitable distribution of wealth and consumption in society as a whole. The definition of the balance of welfare and equity with fairness is an integral part of the language of both national and international politics. As such, it underlies the business environment and market opportunities which exist in specific countries and regions of the world.

The international balance of:

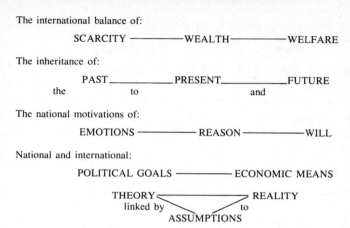

The manager must use his awareness of these concepts as a basis for devising effective and profitable global strategies with application to diverse national and local markets.

Figure 3.1 Some Global Concepts

3.3   The Passage of Time and Risk

Another important line of thinking open to the manager seeking business opportunities within the global business environment is to look at the *dimension of time* as expressed through the passage of commercial events from the past to the present and the future. The development of markets through time and the many uncertainties which surround these processes is a central feature to understanding the nature of markets as a whole. From past inheritances are drawn important business assets. There is the fixed capital for land and financial resources, machinery and markets which have been bequeathed to the company by past generations. Present and future production and planning is based on the rich sources of previously discovered and applied scientific and technical ideas and inventions. For business managers, the present is a time of constant change, linking the inheritances, both physical and intellectual, of the past into the future. As a corollary, the present is concerned with the day-to-day decisions managers must make about production and consumption, and on the depreciation and replacement of assets which this implies. It is essential to put aside savings for an investment programme in order to sustain the production into the future and to enable further consumption to occur.

The future is unknown, and perhaps — in any complete sense — unknowable. Nevertheless, it is essential for practical global managers to think in terms of foreseeable options or possibilities. Inevitably, whatever their business, to some extent they are living in the expectation of future markets. Some businesses, concerned essentially with short-term buying and selling, and day-to-day operations, may be able to operate without taking any elaborate long-term view of the future. However, other businesses, certainly those involved in global markets for major design and investment activities, the planning of great projects, such as building dams, motorways, power stations, or development of new aircraft, will inevitably require long planning horizons into the future. The nature of this future brings us into the realms of *forecasting* and *scenario writing*, to try to make some sense of what is likely to happen, and to devise realistic strategies and plans for future markets in many different parts of the world.

3.4 Motivations of People, Cultures and Countries

Another category of importance is the question of *motivation*, which clearly varies widely from person to person, place to place, and country to country. Individual motivations might be thought to be shaped by a mixture of emotions, which are usually based on past or present experiences, and by an attempt to direct emotions to the application of reason, leading to some future desired goal. Managers operating in global markets are aware that individual countries, societies and cultures are shaped by a blend of emotions about their past inheritance, and about their current role in the world, with the need to apply reason to present circumstances in the pursuance of a variety of national purposes as expressed through a political will. Looking and travelling around the world, the international manager must be highly sensitive to the different elements of *emotions, reason* and *will* which he will inevitably encounter in different countries, or even within regions of the same country. It is only by understanding the basic motivations of people in diverse cultures and the reasons for present activities and future aspirations, that he will be able to begin to develop effective global market strategies as a whole.

3.5   Balance of Political Goals and Economic Means

A further category of thinking involves the highly complicated balance between the political goals of a nation as opposed to its *economic* means. Politics are frequently shaped by emotional feelings but there is also, hopefully, a substantial amount of sound reason and will within the mix. The political direction of a country, and the impact that this has on the way it functions is of great importance to the manager seeking to do profitable business there.

The availability of economic means is also of great importance. These may include many diverse assets, from land and mineral resources to local manufacturing and servicing capacity, the education and training of the population, and existence or otherwise of entrepreneurial skills. All are important in sizing up potentiality in a particular market. The abundant local availability of basic raw materials, such as minerals or forests, is a commercial opportunity for exploitation. However, their absence could also mean that there is a potentially profitable market opportunity to supply such minerals or timber to the local economy.

The international manager, in scanning around the world for such commercial opportunities, needs to look at what is both politically and economically feasible within particular societies, and then decide how his own company's specific blend of resources and skills can be deployed to complement and support and develop profitably the underlying potentiality of diverse local markets in many parts of the world.

3.6   Turning Theories into Global Business Strategies

Thus far we have been thinking at a conceptual level. To make such theories have any meaning for action, it is important for the successful manager to establish realistic assumptions and to balance such assumptions with a viable reality and a profitable outcome. There is no lack of theories about the political organisation of nations, nor about the importance of economic and social ends. None of these have any real meaning for the practical manager unless they can be understood and applied in a practical and effective way. This means translating local national political, economic and social awareness into effective and profitable management actions, policies and strategies. Extending this into the wider risks and opportunities of global markets is what international management is all about.

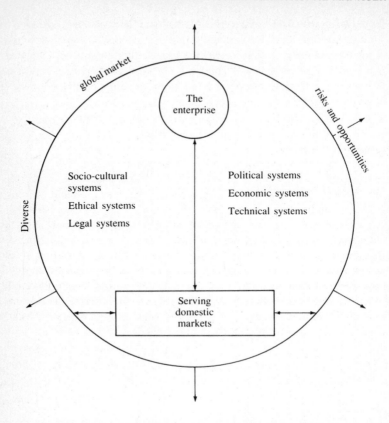

The need for managers is to look outwards to a diversity of international market risks and opportunities

Figure 3.2   The Management of an Enterprise Within Global Business Environments

In taking a view of the opportunities and risks which particular world markets may present for his enterprise, a manager will need to link his perception of global opportunities to a variety of theories about the creation, definition and increase of material wealth and welfare. In this, he immediately comes into contact with fundamental questions about both the potential, and the organisation of diverse national markets in many parts of the world. They will almost certainly include:

(a) Ideas about the ways in which international trade should be organised, and whether the particular economy under review is organised on a *protectionist* or free-trade comparative advantage basis. This reality will have an immediate and direct impact on policies relating to imports and exports, and the establishment of local manufacturing capacity.

(b) A second issue is the existence of fertile land and other finite natural resources. Does the relative scarcity and finiteness of such resources provide a fundamental constraint to further growth, or can new businesses — by the deployment of new techniques, new capital and new scientific ideas — unlock resources in ways hitherto undreamt of?

(c) There are questions about population growth and size, and the availability of skilled labour. What skilled labour is available, how rapidly is it increasing, and in what ways is it employed at the moment? Is it possible, within a particular market, to see an improvement in the way such labour is used and, indeed, an improvement in the employment of such labour within the economy as a whole? What implications does this also have for the growth of effective market demands and consumption?

(d) What is the availability of capital, local and imported, and how is this used in conjunction with technology to promote economies of scale and to enhance industrial productivity and output? What does this mean in terms of competition, actual or potential, between local and overseas firms?

(e) There are many questions about ideas of risk taking and the degree to which a society is open to innovation and change, and to ways of promoting efficiency and growth by competitive or other means.

(f) Another category is involved with market organisation and whether competition is favoured or whether some form of government regulation of markets exists. There is an immense variety of circumstances applying in different countries to market structure, organisation and competition, and it is important for the manager to understand the degree to which competitive methods may be used, or the degree to which new business must fit into local regulatory frameworks or legislation.

(g) The issue which has achieved great prominence in recent times is the availability of secure supplies of energy of all types. Modern economies are highly energy-dependent, and adequate availability and efficiency of its use underpins the way in which societies will function in the future. Energy economics is central to the understanding of the way most economies function, and the opportunities for growth and profits which exist.

(h) What is the local role of money, as a unit of account, as a means of exchange, and as a store of value? What sort of money system does the individual country have, and how does it function? Is the currency freely interchangeable with other currencies, or how does the exchange rate system apply to the remittance of capital payments, of interest and dividends abroad? What impact does taxation have on this?

(i) What are the perceived functions of government and does the government of a particular country adopt an interventionist policy in relation to the market, or follow a more 'hands-off' non-interventionist policy? This in turn inevitably links back to ideas of market organisation, and the regulation for competition and the impact of legislation and taxation as a whole on the ways in which private industry is allowed to function.

(j) Finally, there are the questions of a particular nation's concept of welfare and equity, and of fairness within its society. These affect both opportunities and constraints in the role in which new business initiatives can be applied. Social responsibility questions loom large in the perception of the functioning of multinational companies in many countries.

Sensitivity to all these diverse theories, conditions and circumstances will underlie the ways in which an international manager transposes and enhances his own global awareness into effective local and national strategies for his enterprise. A particular challenge of international operations is that an international manager is having to operate within nations and localities of which he may have little prior knowledge. He has continually to move into new markets in a humble and learning mode, establish sensible ground rules for the local situation, and create company policies which are appropriate for both:

(a) the exploitation of short-term market opportunities, and
(b) the development of longer-term strategic positions for his enterprise.

He is, in fact, continually moving across national boundaries, and through boundaries of ideology and ideas, including the frontiers of past practices, present opportunities, and future hopes. To understand his own individual and national motivations and to compare and contrast them effectively with other individual and national motivations, he must learn a great deal about other people's languages, cultures, aspirations and attitudes. It is essential to learn all this, in order to be able to operate effectively in the international environment, and this calls for personal qualities of a high order. The international manager's task requires great initiative, flexibility, adaptiveness, and what in the last resort might be described as a sense of global vision linked to both individual motivation and commercial awareness and drive.

3.7 Some Corporate Management Questions on Global Competition

1. Does the company's past tell us anything of value about the future?

2. To what extent are the circumstances unique to the company or country as opposed to being part of a wider global situation?

3. How far should we look forward, i.e. duration of trends and cycles:
   (a) Quantitatively: deductive—predictive
   (b) Qualitatively: inductive—scanning?

4. What impact will the new technology have on production world-wide?

5. How far do energy and raw material prices directly influence costs?

6. To what extent are unit labour costs critical?

7. In major domestic markets, will import penetration be important? In main overseas markets, are new possibilities arising?

8. How much are market opportunities, both at home and abroad, influenced by currency exchange rates?

9. To what extent are we creating new world markets, as opposed to substituting for old markets?

10. Is the company's management style to be:
    (a) Innovative
    (b) Reactive?

11. Does this style suit all of the cultures and nations with which we operate?

12. What global assumptions does the company make? Are we:
    (a) Optimistic — bullish: the future is bright
    (b) Pessimistic — bearish: the future is cloudy?

13. What facts do we use:
    (a) Quantitative projection of past and present trends
    (b) Qualitative judgement as to key change points?

14. How do we reconcile all these types of evidence to form judgements for developing globally-based management strategies for the future?

3.8   Some Global Considerations

In Chapter 1 attention was drawn to some global scenarios for the 1990s. The following case studies consider the implications of a number of *global agenda* items for the development of the international economy at large. The same items have specific implications for international and local companies seeking to establish secure and growing markets in these rapidly changing situations.

(a) DEBTS AND THE WORLD DEVELOPMENT CRISES

The problems of runaway population increases, flagging agricultural systems and the needs of most developing countries for more public and private sector infrastructure investment have been referred to in Chapter 2. The scale of global debt and the implications of this debt for the future of international trade provide a *mini*-case study — with *maxi* implications for the future of the global economy as a whole.

At the time of writing some $700 million of global debts are outstanding and many countries are having great difficulty in servicing high interest charges let alone repaying capital. The World Bank 1985 *Development Report* gave particular emphasis to the crucial role which international capital plays in the process of economic development. As the report emphasises, it cannot be seen as something that 'occasionally becomes a crisis needing urgent attention'. The ebbs and flows of international finance are today an essential part of business activity in an interdependent world. The report recognises that debt can become a crisis as the result of the mis-handling of national economic policies over many years.

However, it also points out that international financial links have become much more important than hitherto in determining the economic performances of the developing countries. It goes on to say that the policies of the major industrial countries, particularly in respect of fiscal, monetary and trade matters, largely determine the external climate for the developing countries.

In seeking to analyse the impact of these forces on the developing countries the World Bank represents two medium-term 5-year scenarios for the evolution of the global economy. The period running up to 1990 is described as a period of *transition* for the developing country debt problem. It assumes no cyclical swings in world-wide economic activity even though it recognises that such swings will probably occur. It also assumes no major shocks from unpredictable major disruptions in the supply of energy or other critical commodities. The Bank suggests that all the major industrial countries can make major progress in adapting their economic policies in such a way as to reduce budget deficits and high interest rates which would assist employment and permit a roll back in the tendency towards protectionism. The developing countries could then achieve a smooth transition back to credit worthiness and steady growth. It is considered that such policies in the industrial world could result in global economic growth of some 3.5 per cent between 1985 and 1990. Likewise real interest rates could decline from an average of 6.8 per cent for the period 1980—85 to around 2.5 per cent by the end of the decade.

The Bank, however, goes on to warn that failure by the industrial countries to adopt such policies could result in unemployment rates remaining high and real interest rates still averaging 6.5 per cent, and with economic growth in the industrial countries levelling off to only 2.7 per cent for the period. The result of this type of situation in the major industrial countries would inevitably mean that 'several groups of the developing countries' could find themselves with heavier debt service burdens at the end of the decade than they had at the beginning. In these circumstances, sheer economic survival would replace economic development as a goal for the developing countries. Indeed even the 'middling' developing countries would have to continue to choke back imports and to cut back on investment. This situation would raise questions 'about the ability of social political fabrics in many countries to withstand such continuing pressures'. The Bank considers the position is particularly bleak for many poorer African countries where even the more optimistic economic projections suggest that the best that can be hoped for is a maintenance of the present average per capita incomes.

Central to the assumptions underlining these projections are ideas about global capital flows. The more optimistic projections suggest that net financing flows to developing countries will increase from $72 billion in 1984 to $121 billion by 1990. This would be an average growth rate of 11.6 per cent in capital flows. Likewise, official development assistance is assumed to increase by 2.7 per cent per year which would also provide some scope for increasing financing for the lower income African countries without continuing the current process of cutting back on concessional financing for other lower income countries. Yet it does not believe that these financial flows will be adequate. Private lending, mainly from commercial banks, could be assumed to rise by 13 per cent per year. If, however, the *slower growth, high real interest scenario* prevails, the World Bank estimates that total net financing flows would increase from $72 billion in 1984 to only $82 billion in 1990, a decline in real terms. In such circumstances the need for re-scheduling and pressures for involuntary lending would be greatly increased.

Looking specifically at the problems facing Africa, the International Financial Corporation, an affiliate of the World Bank, recently introduced an African Project Development Facility, which will arrange financial backing for private investors in the continent. This project has the backing of the United Nations Development Programme and agencies of the West German, Dutch and US governments. The IFC is also planning a permanent pool of senior management personnel from private sector concerns which have invested in projects in Africa. Yet all these types of programmes raise deep controversy and strong emotions for policy makers in Africa and many other parts of the developing world as well. On the one hand they are constantly being urged by the Western governments to regard foreign borrowing as a substitute for commercial borrowing. On the other hand the painful reality has been that there has been a serious fall in foreign investment in the developing countries in the mid-1980s and this is likely to persist into the immediate foreseeable future.

Some Management Questions

1. What are the implications for your business of the current levels and distribution of global debt?

2. How should one set about assessing a country's credit rating?

3. What level of financial risk is the company prepared to take

to establish or maintain markets in countries with heavy debt burdens?

4. How can a company spread its risk exposure between different countries' markets and products?

5. Do we have the financial resources to enter or remain in Second or Third World developing-country markets?

(b) THE ONGOING GLOBAL ENERGY CRISIS

Events in the Middle East from the early 1970s onwards brought into sharp focus the critical dependence of the world's industrial system on fresh supplies of energy, both to sustain present levels of activity and to create additional growth in the future. In fact, there has always been an incipient energy crisis lurking behind the idea of diminishing returns from the use of finite natural resources. The history of energy exploitation and utilisation in Great Britain and the other major industrial countries well illustrates this basic theme, and provides a fascinating historical case study of the relationship between energy usage and industrial development and economic growth. The move from depending on human and animal labour to water power and windmills, and thence to wood burning for iron smelting and on to the massive nineteenth-century expansion of the coal industry, is part of the economic, social and political history of first Britain and then other industrial countries as well. During the twentieth century attention has been given to the possible constraint of economic growth by the lack of adequate energy supplies. Experience of shortages during two world wars emphasised this.

The years since World War II have continued to be characterised by a number of different phases of increasingly global energy crises. Well into the 1950s the economic recovery of Western Europe as a whole was held back by its inability to produce sufficient coal for industrial reconstruction and expansion. A pressing problem was lack of sufficient dollars to finance coal imports from the United States. This crisis passed away with the enormous expansion of Middle Eastern oil resources, at highly competitive prices, from the late 1950s onwards. Democratic politicians throughout Europe were apparently able to regard with equanimity the rationalisation and, in many cases, under the aegis of the European Coal and Steel Community, the run-down of their coal-mining industries, and to launch their by now rapidly expanding market economies by a massive dependency on Middle Eastern oil supplies. This was during the post-1956 and Suez period, when the possibilities of direct political or strategic control by the West were being steadily lost or abandoned throughout the Middle East.

In the first decade after the end of World War II Western Europe's main energy source was still more than four-fifths provided by coal and barely one-tenth by oil. By the early 1970s energy consumption, which had nearly doubled in line with the growth of GDPs, was nearly three-fifths derived from oil, much of which was being imported from the increasingly politically unstable Middle East, and just over one-fifth was provided by domestically produced coal. The natural gas industry was also beginning to provide an abundance of energy, increasing to over one-tenth of total European supplies. Hydro-electric power provided a further 3−4 per cent and nuclear power barely any energy at all. Forecasts suggested the possibility that if nothing was done Western Europe would become even more dependent on oil for its basic energy supply and that domestically produced coal would slump to provide barely one-tenth of total supplies. Natural gas production provided the main alternative form of new energy, though nuclear power, supported by a major research and development effort, would gradually be pushed up to an increasing proportion. America's unrestrained growth in energy usage was also forcing her into the world market, to import a larger proportion of her total oil and energy needs from the same Middle Eastern fields on which Western Europe had become so dependent. A further preoccupation was the fear that eventually the USSR would also cease to be a surplus producer of oil and be forced onto the global energy market as a buyer, together with her other COMECON member states.

The onset of the current energy crisis following on from OPEC's quadrupling of oil prices in 1973 and the further doubling of prices in the late 1970s certainly brought back into clearer perspective the longer-term prospect of insufficient fresh energy restricting the continued growth and, indeed, the survival of urban and industrial markets as we know them. Evidence about this critical global interdependency on energy supplies was emphasised by analysis included in the World Bank's *World Development Report, 1979*. On the *global demand side* the most critical feature remained the relationship within different economies of per capita energy consumption (kilograms of coal equivalent) over the period 1960−76. Low income countries on average used very small amounts of energy, the figure rising from 113 to 166 over the sixteen-year period. Middle income countries, many of which were beginning to approach a stage of industrial 'take-off', had a more dramatic increase in their per capita consumption, from 393 to 916 over the same period. The average for the industrial countries had also risen, from 4,462 to 7,079. Within this group the United States, with a per capita energy consumption of 8,172 rising to 11,554, was by far the largest individual user. Amongst the COMECON states, with their centrally planned economies, the average of 1,378 to 2,047 showed a rising trend and within this group the USSR, increasing its average per capita consumption from 2,839 to 5,259, was by far the largest total consumer.

Another set of statistics is also important — the relationship between energy consumption per dollar GDP (kilograms of coal equivalent). This is an important relationship because it suggests a degree of efficiency with which countries are able to use energy to make their economies grow. Historical evidence suggests that as low income countries begin to move towards an industrial 'take-off' phase, they use more energy per capita, and this is supported by the figures of the World Bank Report: 0.9 in 1960 to 1.1 in 1976. A similar trend is apparent with the middle income countries, rising from 0.7 to 1960 to 1.2 in 1976. On the other hand, industrialised countries are becoming slightly more efficient in the use of energy to promote economic growth, with a small fall from 1.2 to 1.1 for the same period. However, the centrally planned economies, with their antiquated technology, widely dispersed industrial bases, heavy armaments programmes and massive construction programmes — often located in remote regions — are extremely profligate in their use of energy in relation to the growth of GDP, the figures being 2.2 in 1960, and still 2.0 in 1976.

On the *global supply side*, the 1979 World Development Report also contained many forebodings of future crises, not in the form of forecasts but rather as illustrations of the magnitudes involved. After 1985 world demand for energy was thought likely to outstrip supply, adding to the upward pressure on prices. Yet come 1988 *this does not seem to have happened*! Slower economic growth and the new abundance of alternative oil and gas supplies and the inability of OPEC to agree on production levels has had the effect of depressing prices. However, given any major global market recovery, energy demands and prices could rise strongly. Any renewed upward pressure on prices would clearly have the most significant meaning for the world's future balance of economic and industrial market activity. In the longer term an expanding global economy probably means that the 'international energy balance' will once again become tight. Certainly any post-Chernobyl power station disaster could trigger a move away from nuclear developments and thus put pressure on other energy supplies.

In these circumstances the energy coefficient between usage and economic growth must remain a critical factor for world market growth as a whole. Any real, or even threatened rise in energy relative to other costs acts as a powerful de-stabilising influence on business confidence within the industrially advanced nations, both OECD and potentially COMECON as well. This has several implications which may be summarised as follows:

(i) At the time of the 1979 Tokyo Conference of heads of the seven major industrial states, it was seen as essential that the major industrial nations should seek to restrict their demands — particularly on oil imports — to present levels. This would mean becoming accustomed to the idea of a very slow growth in per capita incomes or even, as appeared likely, a 'stationary stage' for the time being. This proved to be unpopular with populations and workforces grown accustomed during the 1960s and early 1970s to full employment and ever-increasing real incomes. It was also unpopular with those lower-income and middle-income countries which had also been looking towards increased expectations of affluence for their teeming millions. Faced as they all were with the continued growth in total populations, and the drift of people off the land into urban living, the need for secure energy supplies appeared particularly critical. Nothing has happened since then to change this view.

(ii) More fundamentally, the instability of energy availability and prices clearly has an adverse effect upon the longer term confidence, stability and growth of the world's industrial market systems. In the 1930s the famous British economist J.M. Keynes was able to advocate government intervention and demand management within the Britain of his time because he was able to assume that within existing technology and industry there was a reasonable elastic supply of resources: labour, capital, management, raw materials and, perhaps most critical of all, abundant domestic supplies of coal. However, today it is recognised that even short-term instability and checks in oil supplies (as demonstrated by the conflicts between Iran and Iraq and threats of instability elsewhere) can have the most profound and rapidly mutliplying effects on the continued smooth, confident functioning of the world's economic and industrial systems.

(iii) All the industrial nations are today actively seeking new forms of energy creation, which it is hoped will have the effect of gradually reducing real costs. The critical question is, how long will this process take, and what will be the cost? The very long lead times necessary in the complex chain of exploration, research and innovation actively to produce fresh supplies of energy, must not be overlooked. The British Sizewell inquiry took several years to complete and building a new nuclear power station from scratch will take many more!

(iv) There must also be continued attempts to improve greatly the efficiency of energy usage on a world-wide basis. The industrial countries will need to have reduced their energy coefficients down towards 0.6 per unit of growth of GDP to accommodate the changing availability and price situation, deriving from the run-down of oil resources, and the many costs of expanding alternative coal, gas and nuclear sources of supply, etc.

Yet, uncertain and unstable as the long-term global energy balance often appears, it is by no means a new problem in the history of industrial markets. Energy exploration and usage has continually had to accommodate to man's search for the elixir of growth for all. Past experience suggests that despite the various upsets which have occurred, the long-term story is of man successfully mastering the energy constraints of market growths as they appear. The 'dragon to be slain' in the foreseeable future is still *how* to produce sufficient secure new energy to meet the expectations for improvements in living standards and consumption to which millions of people now aspire. As the world's population rises from nearly five billions today to over six billions by the end of the century, this will remain a major and recurring challenge for global business as a whole.

Some Management Questions

1. How directly dependent is one's own business on the use of finite energy supplies and prices for production?

2. In what ways can the organisation seek to spread the risk of drastic changes in energy prices?

3. To what extent are the markets we serve influenced by energy availability and prices?

4. What policies should government and industry jointly pursue to avoid energy problems in the short and the longer term?

5. How will technology changes influence future energy scenarios?

(c) GLOBAL ARMAMENTS AND WAR AND PEACE

An important part of modern industry and its markets is tied into the world-wide demand for weapons of war. The global military balance and the immense scale of armaments manufacture and trade is a critical element underpinning the industrial scene. The world balance of power and the huge costs of nuclear and conventional weapons are issues underlying all thinking about the foreseeable future. The hopes for continuing détente and the restraint of both international and localised terrorism and violence must be an inevitable part of any scenario of the future.

Since the end of World War II sustained attempts have been made to maintain world peace through the work of the United Nations and its various agencies, and many other regional defensive relationships and alliances. The *Annual Strategic Surveys* of the International Institute for Strategic Studies indicate the contemporary global scene. In the northern hemisphere the North Atlantic Treaty Organisation (NATO) confronting the Warsaw Pact forces symbolises the balance of power. Yet debates at the annual Conferences on European Security have underlined the fragility of present power relationships. The continued rivalry of the two competitive political, economic and social systems, of Western Democratic Capitalism as opposed to Marxist-Leninist Industrial Communism, remains a critical issue. The Soviet invasion of Afghanistan and events in the Horn of Africa, in the Middle East and in Central America show yet again the possibilities of violence escalating. Such acts represent a continuous threat to the possibilities of world political stability and of economic and social improvement and growth.

A vast amount of debate is going on about an appropriate defence stance for the West during the 1980—90s. One example of this type of thinking is a report produced by the Royal Institute of International Affairs under the title of, *Western security: what has changed and what should be done?* (1981). The report included contributions from the directors of the four leading foreign policy institutions of the West: Winston Lord, President of the US Council on Foreign Relations; David Watt, Director of the

Royal Institute of International Affairs in London; Carl Kayser, Director of the German Foreign Policy Institute in Bonn; and Thierry de Montbrial, Director of the French Institute for International Relations in Paris. The context of the report was the apparent continued expansion of Soviet military power and the fact that the old relationship between a dominant America and a fairly passive Europe no longer works. The question arises, what should take its place? Coming out of the report were a number of specific proposals:

(i) A *principal nations* group, consisting of the USA, UK, France, Germany and Japan, should co-ordinate and implement security policy outside the NATO area, starting with the Middle East, from which area the greater part of their oil-based energy supplies now comes. There is a need for regular consultation and contingency planning, and some joint military capability located in that region.

(ii) It was also proposed that the annual summits of the five powers mentioned above, together with Italy and Canada, should be strengthened and supported by a permanent secretariat. This led on to a discussion of the desired and related defence improvements.

(iii) The USA should maintain its strategic nuclear balance and strengthen its capability for world-wide military intervention, while at the same time continuing to pursue the Strategic Arms Limitation Talks (SALT) dialogue with the Soviet Union, etc.

(iv) NATO should stick to its pledge of a 3 per cent annual growth in defence spending, but at the same time be prepared to review in depth all aspects of its current defence posture.

(v) NATO should also pursue the modernisation of theatre nuclear weapons in Europe, in conjunction with East-West negotiations for reduction of Theatre Nuclear Forces (TNF).

(vi) The West should review all aspects of East-West trade and its implications for the security of the Third World.

(vii) Europe and the USA should agree on a contribution to a joint military capability to resist Soviet expansion outside the NATO area.

(viii) Common policies on diplomatic, economic and aid fronts should be devised in conjunction with the military strategy in the Middle East.

Underlying the four directors' 1981 report was the view that a larger European defence commitment to the Middle East would be seen as a *quid pro quo* for a more significant role in the formulation of American policy. The mechanism of this bigger role would be a new institution which would be composed of those countries which are primarily concerned with those major problems facing the West and are prepared to make a full contribution to their solution. Predictably this group of countries should include the USA, Britain, France, Germany and, perhaps less certainly, Japan. The report fails to give adequate emphasis to the degree to which foreign policy problems of the Western countries are closely inter-related with economic problems. While the authors gave attention to the gravity of the economic crisis of the 1980s, they asserted that their main concern should be security issues. Yet it might be argued that the West could do as much for the security of its oil supplies by making a concerted attempt to grapple with the problems created by the prospect of long-term instability of oil prices and the need for debt servicing and continued creative investment in other areas, as by preparing to confront the Russians in the Middle East, in Africa or elsewhere.

Some Management Questions

1. What is the distinction between national defence readiness and general global security?

2. How does our company and country fit into the global defence industry and security situation?

3. Is our company directly involved with major defence contracting or sub-contracting either at home or overseas?

4. If so, what are the major business and national security issues which arise in respect to these markets?

5. What do we envisage to be the major scientific and technological changes influencing the defence industries in the future?

(d) THE ROLE OF COMMODITIES IN INTERNATIONAL TRADE

Commodities have always played an important role in global trade with debate about them ranging from the fear of long-term scarcities and escalating prices on the one hand to the problems of over-production, gluts and weakening prices on the other. In the 1970s the primary concern was that commodities were limited, that the OPEC oil market was setting an example of a successful cartel to other primary mineral producers. The emerging political pressure was for a new international economic order which, it was suggested, would lead to 'fairer' and, presumably, higher prices to commodity producers. The 1980s saw a reversal of these trends with a weakening global oil price and a general surplus and lower prices for the other main commodities, from such finite materials as gold, silver, copper, tin and zinc to the 'reproducibles' such as food grains, soya beans, wool and most other agricultural products entering world markets. Yet the ups and downs of the great world commodity markets remain very important, not least for those developing countries which rely on one or two basic commodities for their export earnings — and without which they are incapable of financing imports of essential fuels and machinery and are also unable to service or repay the debts accumulated so freely in the expansionary boom years of the late 1970s.

Looking at the general factors influencing prices in the major world markets, four major features emerge:

(i) The *exchange rate* effect in a world of floating currencies is of great importance. The US dollar was historically low in the late 1970s and later rose sharply to reach a peak in 1985. It was then some 40 per cent higher in value and this translated directly into dollar commodity prices. This enabled buyers in dollars to acquire commodities more cheaply in their own terms than was previously the case.

(ii) The *demand effect* was influenced by the fact that the global economy grew much more slowly between 1975—84 than in the previous decade. (The difference for the main OECD countries has been estimated to be 2 per cent per annum compared to 5.5 per cent.) Industrially dependent commodities like metals and natural rubber experienced weaker markets than agricultural food products which maintained a more steady growth in demand.

In such changing circumstances the immediate effect of weakening demands is on prices. But, in the longer term the effects of weakening demands and prices shift through into levels of longer-term production and capacity. However, for most commodities investment lags are very long and capacity continues to come on stream after demand and prices have weakened, leading to a tendency to gluts and prices depressing further. This condition certainly applied in the case of many metals. Meantime, for the major agricultural food products, high levels of agricultural support in the USA, the European Community and Japan both keep domestic food prices up and also restrict, through quotas and other means, the opportunities for many less-developed countries to stay in the market. In some cases, global surpluses of food grains and sugar have led to dumping on a global scale and this has further damaged the traditional export markets for less-developed countries.

(iii) A third feature is the impact of *market psychology* which at times becomes gripped with the notion that scarcity and high prices are a normal state of affairs that will persist forever into the future. During most of the boom years of the later 1970s markets became gripped by a concern for limits to economic growth because resources were finite and high prices, as exemplified by the OPEC cartel, would go on increasing into infinity. Computer projections by a group of economists and others known as the Club of Rome suggested the possibility of endless rising prices and, indeed, the literal exhaustion of many key products in the next 50 years. A bleak prospect indeed! The mood of the 1980s has become quite different, with falls in global demand, and over-capacity and collapsing price levels for many products becoming the order of the day.

(iv) A fourth feature is what is happening on the *supply side*, both in the shorter and longer terms. It seems clear that for most commodities, including both finite minerals and reproducible agricultural products, the 1980s have been characterised by a reduction in costs, some of which have come from genuine increases in efficiency by improved methods and machinery and, in other cases, by shorter-term savings such as wage cuts and running down of capital.

Moving away from the underlying features which affect commodity prices towards a more general sense of the fortunes of particular markets, we find many diverse and often conflicting situations. The global purchasing manager concerned with these individual markets has to carefully monitor the 'real world' in both the short and longer term to try to understand and, hopefully, anticipate or predict the trends that will affect his own commodity input prices.

Taking the case of non-ferrous metals it appears that North America is the major producer. In recent times it became a relatively high-cost producer, the cost re-inforced by the high rate of exchange for the dollar. The effect of these cost pressures was to force the closure of old and inefficient plants, to employ new machinery and methods and to impose lower wages. Other high-cost producers of metals exist in the less-developed countries, though in these cases it appears that the public sector companies have often been less successful at reducing costs because of the pressure of social and political circumstances which surround them. Moreover, in most less-developed countries the need for foreign exchange has become so acute that many government-owned agencies have continued to seek to maintain production and exports in the face of collapsing prices. Indeed, in order to try to meet debt-service obligations, producers in less-developed countries have been forced by their governments to maintain and increase exports. This has required lower international prices which can only be achieved through currency devaluation. The pressure to devalue, with all the attendant consequences on a less-developed country's import prices and general living standards, has often come from the IMF during negotiations over international debt repayments.

Looking to agricultural commodities yet other adverse circumstances arise. As we have seen elsewhere, the post-World War II period was characterised by a massive increase in agricultural productivity, especially in the highly scientific and technological agricultural production (and delivery and storage) systems which now operate in North America, Australasia, Europe, Japan and elsewhere. Even in many of the less-developed countries of Asia, the successful application of the 'green revolution' has been to shift the emphasis away from the continuing threat of famine to something approaching sufficiency in most years. However, in some less-developed countries, especially in Africa, the vagaries of climate, slow social changes and adaptation and political ideology, combined with the problems of distance and inadequate transport, mean that acute areas of famine have continued to recur. The result has been a world food grain market characterised by glut and over-production and weakening prices in one place, going hand in hand with famine in other areas. The additional complication of the apparent inability of the Soviet agricultural system to meet its own needs for adequate food grains to feed cattle for meat production has led to acute political difficulties, both within the Eastern Bloc and also in terms of the relationship which the US Government has with its own farming communities (who are anxious to establish secure markets and prices for their food grains on a global basis). Other acute conflicts of over-production and accusations of global dumping of food grains have also flared up between the USA and the EEC, and between the USA and the EEC *vis-à-vis* Australia.

The question which inevitably arises is, who are the winners and who are the losers in the international commodity price casino? At present it appears that the gainers are the major producers and consumers in the major industrial countries. The fall in oil prices has an immediate impact on every motorist and consumer of oil and gas. In turn, this has an effect on coal prices and the wages and employment of miners. The falls in most other major commodity prices, with the possible exception of tin, are not so dramatic, but nevertheless also have their effects on industrial costs and inflationary pressures and living standards. The fall in commodity prices has resulted in a considerable shift in the *terms of trade* in favour of manufacturers and against primary producers wherever they may be located. In the case of less-developed countries, attempts by individual producers to improve their own competitive position have often been to move the terms of trade further against primary products. Those producers who have been able to cut costs have often been able to maintain or even expand production. However, those who have been unable to cut costs have had to live with lower output levels and lower prices.

Some Management Questions

1. To what extent is our business involved directly or indirectly in commodity markets?

2. If we are substantially influenced or involved, *which* commodities, in price or volume terms, are most important to us?

3. How do we normally monitor or offset the risks involved?

4. To what extent can we effectively substitute one commodity for another in our business or production activities?

5. As a producer or seller of products, are we also substantially influenced by specific commodity prices?

4

Analysing Global Opportunity and Risk

4.1 Management Choices for Opportunity and Risk

Taking a view of international opportunity and risk is one of the most crucial tasks facing the global manager. What does he need to know about his own company and its place, both now and in the foreseeable future, within the world market place? Where are the new opportunities arising for its products and services? How does the manager sort out, from his existing portfolio of the world-wide activities, those markets which his company should concentrate on in the future? Even more difficult, how does he decide which markets the company should plan to withdraw from? Even as late as the early 1970s it was still apparent that the typical British manufacturing company exported goods overseas almost as a by-product to what it was already selling in the home market. In most cases, products which had sold well at home were assumed to be likely to sell well abroad. Thus export marketing for many such manufacturing companies was simply a 'derivative' exercise, based on perhaps 80 per cent of the company's production always having gone to secure domestic markets in Britain. Much has happened since then! Most importantly, and in conjunction with Britain's entry into the European Economic Community in 1973, import penetration by many manufactured products soared, and the previously secure home markets for wide ranges of capital and consumer goods, and even services, were rapidly penetrated and taken over by overseas competitors. Today approximately one third of the manufactured goods consumed in the British home market are supplied from overseas. The secure home base for British-made cars and buses, motorcycles, bicycles, domestic appliances and even 'convenience' foodstuffs became subject to keen competition from overseas suppliers. In the

67

meantime the previously secure overseas export markets, particularly in traditional Commonwealth countries, also succumbed to both intensified competition from local suppliers and massive new competition from America, West Germany, France and Japan. More recently, other major new export competitors have arisen in the newly industrialising nations of the Third World, from South Korea, Taiwan, Hong Kong, Singapore, Malaysia, India and elsewhere.

One important characteristic of much of this new intensified global competition is the way it has been focussed precisely to particular markets and needs. The Japanese multinational companies working through the formidable combination of financially highly-geared, high-technology factories, and linked to world markets through the powerful trading houses, were rapidly able to identify specific market needs, through sophisticated market research programmes. These were linked back, through research and development, into highly automated and efficient production runs geared to potential market demands for specifically designed products. The policy of *concentrating on key markets* and of focussing production and marketing efforts so as to take as much as possible of that expanding market on a global basis paid off handsomely. Throughout the 1970s and 80s Japanese industry conquered the world for entire ranges of motor vehicles, household consumer goods and electronic equipment of all kinds. American, British and many Western European multinational manufacturing companies reeled under this highly structured and focussed marketing attack, and in many cases were obliterated from the market place.

The concentration of Japan's industrial capacity on to *key global markets* and the subsequent exploitation of this breakthrough, presented an immense challenge to manufacturers throughout the Western World.

One response was to try to play the Japanese at their own game. This required major manufacturing and exporting groups to totally re-define their corporate missions, to withdraw resources from thin and widely scattered marketing positions and to let go those products and services for which there was limited demand and low returns. In fact for many British companies it may be suggested that some 80 per cent of their profit came from the 20 per cent of their product markets in which they had a strong position and were able to earn a high rate of return. For the international markets for the future the policy was to concentrate on those *key markets* in which the company was strongly based and leave the more marginal low return markets to other suppliers. While the logic of this strategy seems irrefutable, the reality of the practice is not quite so easy. Few companies have the degree of market knowledge about their present profile of activities, let alone their future possibilities on a global basis, to make such bold decisions quickly with absolute certainty or confidence. Nevertheless in the highly competitive global markets of today a start has to be made somewhere. *Internal knowledge* by the company of its present production and costs, and its future possibilities can only be acquired by senior management deciding on the need for a detailed analysis of where the company is at present, and where it can realistically plan to go in production and marketing terms in the future. However, looking beyond the company also means considering the world as a whole, and where the company stands in relation to particular markets within the global scene, and which markets it should be planning to get into for a new future. This brings the international manager to the hard point of deciding what, in terms of his business, *he needs to know about the world*, and how to set about getting this information in order to plan for new markets.

4.2   Fact Finding and Sources of Information

Any company even marginally engaged in international trade should have within itself a great deal of basic information, which will need to be gathered and assessed on a regular basis. An international manager must be given responsibility for this. He should compile updated summaries of the information which is regularly coming in from internal company sources, especially from reports of overseas subsidiaries and agents. Other useful sources of information include: the systematic reading of quality newspapers from Britain and abroad and other press reports; the compilation of press cuttings by identified subjects; the gathering of product and market information through trade associations, specialised trade bodies and government departments, including the British Overseas Trade Board, and from trade representatives and Commissions abroad. Equally helpful can be the trade officials of foreign embassies and Commonwealth High Commissions in London and the UK offices of the EEC. There is no lack of background information: the basic problem for most companies is first to decide what they need to know for their business and second who is to collect it and report on a regular basis to the relevant managers within the organisation. Who needs to know what becomes a critical issue in deciding sound information collection and dissemination policies.

A logical sequence of information collection for an international company should be as follows.

(a) First identify the basic international data requirements of the company and its products, both now and in the immediate future.

(b) Carefully select and maintain those global data sources which are relevant to the company's marketing and product needs. Regularly review these data sources in terms of their changing content and availability and in the light of what the company's own changing needs are likely to be in the future. Avoid collecting information which is no longer relevant to the company's needs.

(c) Continually check the availability of *new* data. Many new sources of on-line computer-based information are becoming available and, in theory at least, should be more up-to-the-minute than much of the information that has traditionally been available from libraries. Yet while much new on-line data may be available, just how much of it is, in fact, specific enough to the company's needs to be worth paying for on a regular basis?

(d) Exercise continuous vigilance concerning the reliability of information being gathered or surveyed. While statistical collection in most Western countries is reasonably accurate there are often strange inconsistencies comparing one country with another. Thus the question of the useful comparability of data and its interpretation needs to be given constant attention. In many smaller countries markets tend to be monopolised by one or at best a few local producers, while in other markets production may be entirely the domain of state-owned enterprises. In both cases there may be substantial combinations and omissions in the presentation of national production statistics. It may also prove to be difficult to compare realistically the domestic production of goods with main import categories. The categorisation of many import/export items into broad bands of goods may also lack the degree of precision necessary for accurately defining a company product. Thus in many cases it will be necessary to commission or undertake special local market research appraisals to find the relevant facts. Very similar considerations also apply when comparing statistics of 'living standards' between countries. While the World Bank, the OECD and the EEC are all trying to standardize the collection of national statistics as much as possible, nevertheless the very real underlying differences between societies often make generalised comparative statistics about them suspect. The words *reliability, interpretation* and *comparability* must always be in the forefront of the mind of managers using such comparisons as the basis for company global export plans.

The following section indicates some of the major providers of information about political, economic and social trends. They extend over a wide range, from the regular publications of the Organisation for Economic Co-operation and Development in Paris (OECD) to the International Monetary Fund (IMF) and the World Bank in Washington and on to the various agencies of the United Nations including the International Labour Organisation (ILO) in Geneva and the Food and Agricultural Organisation (FAO) in Rome. Likewise, company annual reports, papers by brokers and industry associations are all important. Most of these types of organisations produce regular publications which will repay detailed research and investigation.

Some major sources of published information include:

1. *Commentary on economic/political affairs*
   OECD, Directories such as Europa/Statesmen, Peers, etc.
   IMF Reports and Papers
   World Bank, IBRD (International Bank for Reconstruction and Development)
   ILO (International Labour Organisation)
   National governments' sources of all types
   Foreign embassies, libraries and press releases
   EIU (Economist Intelligence Unit) publications
   EEC publications
   BOTB (British Overseas Trade Board) publications
   Company commentaries and reports (e.g. Shell, Unilever, Exxon)
   Major bank reviews
   Brokers' newsletters
   Press cuttings
   CIA (Central Intelligence Agency) publications
   Consultants

2. *Information on financial corporate affairs*
   Company annual reports/UK
   Brokers' reports
   Companies House/Stock Exchange

Industry association reports
Extel cards
McCarthy
Stock exchanges reports
Capital International
Chambers of Commerce and Industry

3. *United Nations Monthly Bulletin of Statistics*
Year books
FAO (Food and Agricultural Organisation) statistics
IMF and IBRD financial statistics
Government financial statistics
Balance of payments statistics
Trade directories
Some main publications, annual reports, outlooks, surveys, etc.

4. *OECD statistical sources*
Country surveys
Economic outlook
Foreign trade statistics
Labour force statistics
National accounts
Employment outlook

5. *UK Central Statistical Office monthly trends*
Economic trends
Financial statistics
Department of Employment Gazette
British Business
Trade statistics
Annual abstract
Social Trends
Blue Book
Census reports
Bank of England Quarterly, etc.

4.3   Looking at Countries and Markets Overseas

Thus far we have reviewed some of the approaches and indicated some
of the sources which are available to the international manager to assist
him to begin to take a view of new market opportunities abroad. In

approaching a market for the first time some substantial preliminary desk research is desirable, before the natural human desire to rush off and have a look takes over.

Having surveyed the literature and talked to as many knowledgeable people as possible the next step is for the manager to begin an analysis of the business environment in the country or region in which his/her company is considering developing a potential market. It is advisable to take a broad view of the particular *economy* under consideration before focussing enquiries on the specific circumstances and needs of the particular *product* under review. For the initial 'broad-brush' look at the country, the statistics contained in the Appendices of the *World Development Report* (published annually by the World Bank) give a comprehensive, reasonably up-to-date range of country comparisons. These comprehensive and comparative world country statistics may then be supplemented by more selective reading of country reports produced by the major trading banks and organisations like the Economist Intelligence Unit and also from information obtained from the trade experts at foreign embassies, High Commissions, trade associations and the BOTB. The following simple check-list should help in sorting out data about the general state of the economy, its present structure and management by government. The manager should always:

(a) Identify his main data and information requirements.

(b) Select the sources of data and information which commonsense suggests are appropriate to his needs.

(c) Check the availability of the information.

(d) Question the reliability and look at alternative interpretations, and

(e) Cross-check the validity of the comparisons that are being made.

4.4 Assistance from British Government Agencies

For British businessmen involved in international trade the major source of governmental support is provided by the British Overseas Trade Board, whose head office and major information library and other resources are located at 1 Victoria Street, London SW1H 0ET. The Board also operates through ten regional offices and has sixteen Area Advisory Groups, which are responsible on a geographic basis for providing detailed advice on major trading opportunities overseas.

The BOTB is in fact a co-operative venture between business and government. It draws on the advice of leading businessmen, who are members of the Board. The Board guides and directs the government's assistance programmes to exporters and export promotion services and also provides practical help to new, individual exporters. The different types of support currently provided range from financial assistance to exhibiting at overseas trade fairs: they include advice on particular overseas markets; market research abroad; overhead costs of moving into new markets, etc. In addition, specific individual advice can come from 200 British diplomatic posts abroad. They can provide guidance on selling particular goods and services to individual markets abroad and 'on the spot' information about specific overseas companies and their potential as agents.

Among the BOTB services currently available, of particular value to international managers is the Export Intelligence Service, which provides a computerised daily service to subscribers. Export intelligence includes overseas inquiries for products and services, calls for tender, agents seeking UK principals and early notification of prospects overseas. Other useful services which vary from time to time include financial assistance with overseas export marketing research, and financial and other assistance with Inward and Outward Trade Missions. The latter service assists groups of exporters, sponsored by approved trade associations or Chambers of Commerce. Other forms of assistance cover overseas projects under the Aid and Trade Provisions (ATP). The purpose is to import orders to developing countries in which the UK does not normally provide aid, or where the planned allocation is already committed. The scheme is intended to enable Britain to match aid-assisted foreign credit facilities. Other services include an overseas project fund to assist major British contractors for major capital projects overseas, and the World Aid section, which is an initial point of contact for UK exporters seeking information about projects financed by international lending agencies. An Overseas Status Report service enables exporters to obtain an up-to-date view of potential overseas agents and partners. The BOTB has also been active in promoting overseas seminars and encouraging attendance at important trade fairs overseas. In all of these activities the major purpose is to encourage and facilitate as much as possible British competitive strength in global markets.

Another important government service for exporters is the Export Credit Guarantees Department (ECGD) which, together with the banking system as a whole, does a great deal to assist overseas trade through specific credit financing and insurance arrangements.

The ECGD currently provides credit insurance for about one-third of Britain's export trade and insures exporters of both goods and services against non-payment by overseas buyers. The main risks covered include insolvency or protracted default of the buyer, governmental action which stops the British exporter receiving payment, new import restrictions, and war or civil disturbance in the buyer's country. Cover may commence from the date of shipment or from the date of contract (at higher premiums).

This insurance may be supplemented by guarantees of repayment given direct to banks financing exports sold on credit of two years or more, whether in sterling or in foreign currencies. Alternatively, for contracts over £1 million, the ECGD will guarantee loans direct to overseas buyers enabling them to pay on cash terms, or 'lines of credit' similarly covering an agreed buying programme of an overseas country. The banks provide finance against these guarantees. The ECGD is also prepared to support the issue of performance bonds in the commercial market in respect of cash or 'near-cash' contracts worth over £250,000.

Investment insurance is provided for new British investment overseas against expropriation, war damage and restrictions on remittances.

Having reviewed the economy and its potential business environment in these 'broad-brush' terms the manager is now in a position to take a more specific look at the exporting possibilities for his own products and services. He is therefore moving from the general background survey to the more particular operational aspects of his work. The following checklists should help in sorting out the right questions to ask about this difficult process, in both qualitative and quantitative terms.

4.5 Check-List for Analysis of the Current Economic Situation

(a) Present Structure of the Economy

GNP (in $)
GNP per head
Rate of growth of GNP (over a recent period)
Allocation of resources (%):

expenditure on consumer goods and services
expenditure on public consumption
fixed capital investment
stocks
exports
imports
Total government expenditure (% of GNP)
Taxation (% of GNP, sources)
Public ownership (extent, industries nationalised)
Expenditure on social welfare
Regional imbalances

(b) Management of the Economy and Government Policies

Main economic objectives
Level of employment/unemployment
Inflation rate (over a recent period)
Policy on balance of payments:
  surplus/deficit current account
  surplus/deficit capital account
Policy on prices and incomes
Policy on imports and exports (goods and capital)
Policy on taxation
Policy on money supply and monetary controls
Policy on foreign investment — inward and outward
Policy on regional imbalances in the economy

(c) The Evaluation of an Economy and Understanding How It Works

Consideration of the *quantitative* facts about the structure and management of an economy, as listed in headings (a) and (b) above, should give the manager some indication of the way an economy currently works and is influenced by government policies. However, in using this information for decision-making, it is desirable to consider a further dimension to achieve some understanding of how an economy is shaped by more *qualitative* economic, political and social forces, of how these have influenced the present, and how they will affect future performance. To this end, the next check-list can be useful in evaluating how an economy functions and changes over time and the market opportunities and risks it is likely to produce.

4.6 Check-List to Evaluate How an Economy Functions and Changes Over Time

	Past Pattern	Present Situation	Future Probabilities
(a) *Proportions of employment and production in:* agricultural, manufacturing, mining services, etc.			
(b) *Role and motivation of consumers:* urban and rural			
(c) *Role and motivation of producers:* urban and rural			
(d) *Market structures and competition:* number of consumers and producers, product diversity, freedom of entry and information, freedom of choice *vis-à-vis* price and quality			
(e) *Ownership and allocation of means of production:* e.g. land (rent), labour (wages), capital (interest) and entrepreneur (risk/profit)			
(f) *Role and influence of government:* e.g. law, order, defence, macro-management of the economy, ownership and control of production and/or distribution			

(g) *Role of money:*
as a means of exchange
and/or store of value _____

(h) *Trade dependency and
policies:*
e.g. relating to imports,
exports, invisibles _____

(i) *Other considerations:*
degree of economic or
social development (e.g.
subsistence agriculture and
low income as opposed to
highly industrial, urbanised
and high income) _____

(j) *Finally, what type of
economy are we
considering:*
free-market, mixed or
centrally-planned? _____

4.7   Check-List of Some Ways of Looking at Specific Overseas Export Markets

(a) First Assess your Strengths and Weaknesses Against the Needs of your Products and Services

  (i)   Do these products/services suit local market tastes?
  (ii) What will be their position relative to actual or potential competitors?
 (iii) How will your company's pricing strategies work in the overseas market?
 (iv)   What do you expect in terms of financial performance?
  (v)   How much of a lead do you have over the competitors?
 (vi)   What is the degree of special design or service or supply guarantees needed?

(b) Present Company Systems

  (i) What is your company's ability to sustain its lead?

(ii) What distribution channels are or will become available to you?

(iii) Can you achieve control over local dealers and sales forces?

(c) Management Skills and Staff Organisation Required

(i) How will your company recruit experienced local personnel?

(ii) Where will critical skills come from (locally or expatriate)?

(iii) How do you see this particular overseas market in the overall corporate plan?

(iv) How co-operative are present corporate staff and operating divisions to shape their support to the new overseas markets' competitive environment?

(v) What are the company's financial expectations and over what time horizon?

(vi) How much risk can the company accept in the new overseas market?

(vii) How flexible is the company to share certain operating responsibilities and/or functions/business systems with overseas partners?

(viii) Do you have sufficient company support on the above answers across the board and with your major shareholders and other stakeholders?

(d) Some Possible Policy Options with Opportunities and Risks

(i) *To license the product or service to a local partner*
This probably provides a secure short-term, profit-generating decision but potentially provides no long-term advantages.

(ii) *Use a good local agent*
This provides low initial entry costs but affords little long-term control.

(iii) *Establish a physical presence by direct investment*
This will involve the company in direct control and heavy 'up front' costs.
   It also raises the risks of mismanagement, if it is not tailored to the local key factors for success.

(iv) *Form a joint venture with a local partner*
This calls for a balancing of complementary and supplementary strengths and weaknesses so that the whole equals more than the sum of its parts.

It is potentially difficult to communicate or to control.
It requires good communication at all levels of management
and matching company cultures and philosophies.

4.8   Moving from Exporting to Investing Overseas

So far we have been primarily concerned with the ways in which an international manager might look at overseas countries in terms of their market
potential for direct exports of his company's goods and services. Yet,
as the policy options on the previous check-list indicate, a company may
move from the function of exporting itself towards the idea of establishing
a local physical presence in the form of investing in agents and their
facilities, by building factories and other plants and by possibly going
into involved joint ventures and licensing arrangements with local partners. In diverse ways any of these activities can soon lead an exporting
company forward to the idea of putting substantial investment capital
into a country distant from its own. Indeed, today, the world-wide
existence of strong governmental pressures and policies to promote the
creation of local manufacturing capacity and employment capabilities
means that exporting companies are soon moved to considerations of
this sort, once their direct exports have increased to take a significant
proportion of a local market. This puts the company on to the increasingly hazardous tight-rope of making foreign investment decisions, both
in terms of sending investment capital to a country for the building of
local plant and/or of using retaining profits and accumulated capital in
offshore locations for further extension of local production capabilities.

  In previous chapters some of the longer term strategic issues of the
present global business environment were considered. In company
investment terms perhaps the key elements for *practical* decision making
are:

(a) The reality of *unstable political conditions* in many parts of the
    world. More importantly, uncertain political conditions often go
    hand-in-hand with rapid changes in policies affecting trade and
    overseas investment conditions. This has been manifest in many
    places from Iran to Argentina, Nigeria to South Africa.

(b) Changes in host country attitudes and policies towards multinational
    companies and foreign investment. In practical terms the main
    worries for the potential overseas investor are changes impacting

on equity ownership and the repatriation of profits and other funds. Their fear of being locked into a 'sinking ship' situation is very real and best avoided if at all possible!

(c) Exchange rate fluctuations which in the past decade have often made a nonsense of company planning for potential returns on earnings or funds in different parts of the world. Between 1979−87 the $ to £ sterling relationship alone fluctuated over an immense range, from $2.45 to the £1 in 1980 to nearly $1 to £1 four years later and back to $1.82 to the £1 in the middle of 1988. All major trading currencies have experienced huge variations during the post-Bretton-Woods, floating-exchange-rate period. Learning to live with these changes by using the banking system to buy and sell currencies on a forward basis has become a central part of international trading life.

(d) Widespread tendencies to many new forms of protectionism affecting the free flow of goods and services. In some areas there has been a vast extension of so-called non-tariff barriers to trade, ranging from local food and drink regulations through to professional entry standards. These types of constraint are often used to cancel out many of the benefits of the freer trading world brought in by the GATT during the postwar 'golden age' of growth.

(e) The very high level of indebtedness in many of the less developed countries and the suggestion by some, notably Mexico and Brazil, that they may simply suspend payments to overseas lenders, notably the American and Western European Banking System.

Yet despite these very real elements of risk it is also true that for many companies, especially for those based in the highly competitive markets of the West, breaking into new opportunities abroad has also proved to be the route to new profits. Thus great opportunities as well as risks are very much part of the present global business scene. However, in looking at overseas investment opportunities, especially in Third World countries, financial analysis on its own has proved inadequate. Thus there is a strong management interest in other means of looking at the problem of whether or not to invest in a particular overseas market.

In a Stanford Research Institute paper on *Evaluating Uncertainties in Foreign Investment* by Jacobson and Nelson a number of clear steps are proposed:

(a) Companies first need to establish a basic screening procedure in order to ascertain 'the most appropriate countries for their development needs'. The focus is on the company and its international needs rather than on country analysis and profiles as such.

(b) It is important for an international company to apply or develop planning procedures in order to understand how particular foreign investment decisions fit into the global corporate strategy as a whole.

(c) Investments should be defined in the broadest sense — the objective being for the company to be able to maximise such factors as 'profits, revenues and sales, as well as minimise losses'.

(d) In terms of developing or applying such a system for its own use the company should keep in mind the need for *breadth, simplicity and flexibility* to cover the many variables of political, economic, financial, social and cultural data which may be relevant.

(e) Conditions of opportunity and risk vary enormously from industry to industry and country to country. Mining groups with large holes in the ground and long periods of pay-back are in a very different position from a typical manufactuirng or servicing operation which may look forward to recovering its initial overseas investments in a three- to five-year period.

(f) A related issue is that relationships between individual multinational companies and between host governments vary greatly. Some companies, because of their historical position and structure, are in a much better bargaining position than others. Likewise relationships between major international companies and host governments are also influenced by the political relationships between states, which change from time to time and place to place. US companies in Iran, British companies in Argentina and Nigeria, French companies in Australia and New Zealand, all have, in recent times, been strongly affected by an adverse political climate.

(g) For these reasons large multinational companies need to 'put their eggs into more than one basket'. Thus they are interested in developing and applying *screening procedures* to make decisions as to costs and desirable rates of return for choosing between different countries for specific investment projects.

(h) As has already been emphasised the quality of statistical information, especially as applied to business and market potential, varies widely. Thus any attempt at country screening must involve looking at both such 'objective' quantitative factors about market size and potential as exist, and also such features as international debt and ability to repay.

(i) For many multinationals a particular concern in the 1970s and 80s has been the growth of disputes between multinational companies and host governments, particularly in Third World countries, leading to the actual or threatened expropriation of company assets, with minimal offers of compensation in many cases. Most of the less developed countries having achieved political independence see as a logical next step the extension of commercial independence.

The multinational company, in its overseas investment planning, must inevitably balance the potential advantages of a closer in-depth involvement within such countries, with the possibility that the political climate of opinion may shift against it and it will be faced with the loss of its assets. Perhaps the trump card, which many multinationals can offer host countries in the Third World, is the possibility of training and employment for their people linked to improved access to the markets and the technology of the Western World.

4.9 Some Approaches to Overseas Investment Appraisal

Earlier in the chapter we looked at three basic *check-lists*, the first two being concerned with a quick survey of the quantitative and qualitative background of the individual country and the third a way of moving forward to analyse a specific export marketing opportunity. Escalating up the scale of company involvements overseas to consider the possibility of a major investment requires much the same approach. However, given the potential importance of the decision to the company's future, a more prolonged and elaborate procedure is justified. All generally require the company to set up a regular monitoring procedure of conditions overseas and suggest some methods of sifting out alternative proposals about investing in different parts of the world. The majority of such procedures suggest some system of listing key factors down a vertical axis and a number of alternative countries along the horizontal axis. The Stanford Research Institute paper on *Evaluating Uncertainties in Foreign Investment* (1980) highlights the key factors concerning *risk, business climate* and *special factors* which are then rated on a numerical scale 1 to 5 with 1 being 'very unfavourable' and 5 being 'very favourable' and 3 as 'average'. It suggests that under *political risk* fifteen separate categories might be considered in detail, rating and comparing them in several different countries under review. These are:

   (i) Government stability
  (ii) Governmental legitimacy
 (iii) Possible changes in leadership
 (iv) Administrative competence
  (v) Corruption
 (vi) Internal conflict
(vii) Domestic tensions
(viii) Terrorism
 (ix) Regional stability
  (x) External conflicts
 (xi) National resentments and grievances
(xii) Official attitudes towards foreign investment
(xiii) Prospects for nationalisation
(xiv) National finance
 (xv) Labour union power

The next stage of the analysis looks at what is described as *business climate* and includes a wide range of political, economic, social, technological and other related issues. In many ways they are similar to the questions covered in the earlier check-lists, though as they are involved with the possibility of a major investment decision, they need to be examined in somewhat greater detail and graded more rigorously. The main suggested items for *business climate* include:

   (i) Gross National Product (GNP)
  (ii) Patterns of government spending
 (iii) Balance of payments
 (iv) Export and import controls
  (v) Inflation
 (vi) Exchange rates
(vii) Price levels and controls
(viii) Repatriation of funds
 (ix) Company taxes
  (x) Equity ownership
 (xi) Opportunities for expansion
(xii) Competition

(xiii) Absence of restrictions against host country
(xiv) Host country membership of substantial groups
 (xv) Environmental regulations.

Host Government general regulations impacting on business:

   (i) Enforceability of contracts
  (ii) Local availability of raw materials
 (iii) Availability of adequate energy and water supplies
 (iv) Physical infrastructure   ⎱ Supportive of
  (v) Communication facilities ⎰ business need
 (vi) Banking services
(vii) Availability of local capital
(viii) Labour availability and skills
 (ix) Labour productivity
  (x) Labour costs
 (xi) Labour regulations
(xii) Living conditions
(xiii) Cultural conditions (between overseas company and host culture)

The category of *special factors* then becomes a catch phrase to include any issues that have particular relevance to the company undertaking the survey.

While the general listings under risks and business climate can have some general applicability to almost any enterprise looking at investment choices between countries, it is obvious that companies are different, and they all have special needs and special requirements for success: these can only be decided by senior management itself.

This leads one on to some general points about *management assumptions*. Clearly, in undertaking an investment appraisal of this type it is very important for the company to have decided on its overall corporate objectives in terms of overseas investment in general. What may be an acceptable risk for one organisation, given its overall balance of activities and resources, may not be acceptable to another. Changing trends in communications, distribution and technology may rapidly open up global opportunities which simply did not exist before. Thus before any detailed market analysis begins comparing company opportunities in a number of different overseas locations, it is important for the company to establish at the highest level what the new initiative is seen as accomplishing within the general framework of *corporate goals*. Having done this the enquiry then leads on to a number of basic questions:

(a) What is the present business and how would a new business opportunity overseas fit into this pattern?

(b) What impact will the proposed expansion overseas have on existing company activities at home and abroad? What conflicts of interest are likely to occur?

(c) In what direction should the first move be? Does cultural affinity or cultural distance matter in terms of the new opportunity? Does geographic distance from the main home base matter? Does the company and its products require a certain GNP or standard of living to apply before it can fit its production and products into an overseas market?

(d) Over what time scale is the move planned and what is the balance of planning time, to build-up of capacity and production?

(e) How far down the road of licensing, local manufacture or joint venturing, etc. is the company prepared to go, and over what time period will these changes take place?

(f) What product considerations apply? Are the products already sold in other parts of the world acceptable, or is substantial development called for to fit them to the needs of the new market?

(g) What are the main financial requirements in terms of rates of return and capital needs over time?

(h) How does technology fit into the new proposal? Will 'high' technology or 'low' technology fit into the market? Who will decide about this and, most importantly, are there any particular local pressure groups from labour or government favouring particular types of technology and labour intensity?

(i) How does the company's present management style and structure fit into the local scene? Will it be feasible to send out expatriate managers or can locals be brought into the company system?

(j) What sort of local competitive environment exists and does this fit with the company's existing ideas of how things should be done? In many countries the problem of pre-payments or bribes to local officials is an endemic part of commercial practices, and this situation may fit uneasily with the company's ways of doing business at home.

Consideration of these types of question brings into the open the *special factors* which apply to the company in its basic culture; this should indicate the ways in which it will need to modify itself in order to fit into a new investment opportunity overseas. There is obviously no absolutely right or wrong way of doing things. Rather, it is a matter of applying commonsense to devising sensible procedures and policies to meet challenging and diverse needs.

4.10 The Practice and Procedures of Global and Country Market Assessment

So far we have considered some of the major factors that will influence a company in taking a view of world-wide opportunity and risk for its products and services. We have also examined a number of approaches and check-lists that can assist the international manager to consider the state of individual economies. We have also outlined the export opportunities and choices of policies that may apply and the steps, both theoretical and practical, which he will need to go through in the move from exporting to full-scale investment in an overseas location. Throughout, the importance of relating the company's needs and culture to the highly varied and diverse circumstances of individual countries and their markets has been emphasised.

In order to go through these complex stages and choices in a reasonably systematic way the company will almost certainly set up a *project team*. It will be essential for this team, which will include representatives from the main functional areas of the company (finance, production, marketing, sales and personnel), to obtain from senior management a clear brief of the *terms of reference* for its activities and the overseas development goals it is meant to pursue. In particular, the project team will need to have a clear view of those special factors or circumstances that underlie the way the company operates and the particular needs of its existing production, distribution and marketing processes.

For example, an American or Japanese company planning a new investment within the twelve-nation EEC will need to have a very clear idea of how the company's special needs can be accommodated within the still highly varied conditions that apply in the different member countries and regions of the combined Community. While, in theory, internal trade within the European Community is free of tariff barriers, in practice a host of so-called non-tariff barriers to trade still inhibits the free flow of goods and services within the Community markets. Looking beyond the Community to possible additional export market opportunities in Eastern Europe or the Middle East will almost certainly present other issues of a political nature. Each of the EEC's member states still conducts a separate political relationship with overseas countries, and the nature of this dialogue can have a profoundly beneficial or adverse effect upon attempts at exporting from one country within the Community to another country outside the Community.

For promoting links with Eastern Europe, West Germany, with its special trade relationships with East Germany, may be a good location. However, for many parts of the Middle East or Francophone Africa, France makes more sense. Britain also has special trade advantages and disadvantages applying in different regions of the world.

Other considerations, which also need to be clearly established with senior management, are the policies towards sending staff and their families abroad for comparatively long postings, and how they will fit local circumstances. Certainly many American and, perhaps surprisingly, Japanese multinational companies have found locating in Britain makes good sense, because they have found it comparatively easy for their nationals to settle down to life in an English-speaking country. Other related considerations include the availability or otherwise of matching skills in the host country or the ease with which an overseas company can move into the new location, establish a satisfactory local presence, develop and train local staff, and fairly quickly phase out most of its own expensive expatriate staff.

Another important concern that the project teams will need to be fully briefed on is the *underlying logic* of the company's overseas expansion strategy. In some cases this is fairly easy to define. For instance, a mining company, which is reaching the end of exploiting a particular natural resource, will almost certainly be looking around the world for new and economic sources of supply. Thus in the 1960s many world mining groups, which had hitherto operated in Africa and South America, were attracted to Australia because changes in federal government regulations made the export of bauxite possible for the first time, and also because the immense growth of the Japanese industrial economy promised a huge market for iron ore. Other exploitations of Australian coal, gas and oil resources soon followed. The logic of mineral cost and availability and of market needs made such a move a well-nigh inevitable development at that time.

However, for many companies the corporate decision to move into new foreign investment ventures for manufactured capital and consumer goods provides no such clear choice and, often, complex international considerations and motivations apply. In the 1950s many American manufacturing companies decided to establish plants in Western Europe. For the first time the considerations included the pent-up demands arising from post-war reconstruction under the stimulation of the Marshall Aid being provided at that time by the USA to Western European countries.

Another consideration was that many American consumer goods companies were already experiencing heightening competition and market glut in their own domestic markets, and were anxious to find new and potentially more profitable opportunities overseas. The strength of the dollar against the major European currencies also made it economical for American companies to invest in these markets, many of which also provided potential access to other overseas markets as well. Thus an investment in new plant, and the establishment of markets in Britain also presented a golden opportunity for breaking into hitherto protected Commonwealth and Empire markets, from which American producers had been effectively excluded.

Thus the overall circumstances were very favourable, but the problem still remained for American companies investing in Europe, in which countries actually to locate. The development of the seven-nation European Free Trade Area and the six-nation European Common Market was offering future possibilities of open markets over wider areas. However, it was to be almost two decades before the much larger market of the European Economic Community was to come substantially into being, linking as it now does twelve nations and three hundred and sixty million consumers into an increasingly unified, if still highly diversified, market area.

In the 1950s all the Western European states were actively pursuing regional policies to favour new industrial activity in poorer areas with high unemployment, and this ranged from many poorer locations in Southern Italy, rural France and Ireland, to areas of long-term industrial decline in Belgium, Holland and Britain. Other areas with favourable tax and other inducements to investment were the eastern border regions of Western Germany. Thus the incoming multinational company faced a bewildering variety of issues, from market size to product suitability through to the relative attractions of many possible alternative manufacturing locations. There sprang up a substantial consultancy business, often working in conjunction with national and local government agencies, seeking to induce or steer companies into particular locations. As it turned out most of the American multinational companies which came to Western Europe at that time thrived and, in fact, became significant sources of new ideas, technology and products from the new world to the old. Consumer tastes became Transatlantic, and American-style household appliances, the widespread use of motor vehicles, the introduction of jeans and other casual clothing, the extension of convenience food and eating habits, all became part of post-war Western European prosperity.

Later, the impact of European tastes on these goods and services strengthened and, in many cases, the American multinationals were, by the 1970s, communicating many of these tastes and products back into their own domestic market; and they were also facing strong competition from Western European companies who had by this time undertaken a reverse invasion of the US home market. The Volkswagen car and the European sports car from MG, Jaguar, Ferrari and Mercedes found competitive places in America's consumer tastes.

Other special factors and considerations have applied to construction and engineering industry consultants and companies working in worldwide locations, usually linking back to the head office based in America, Britain or one of the other major Western European countries. Historically, many of the American multinational engineering and construction companies had expanded southwards into Latin America and westwards to the Pacific. The British companies had spread to the Middle East and their old colonial empires of Africa and Asia. The French, Belgian and Dutch companies also operated in their respective spheres of influence. Most such companies were usually strongly ethnocentric in character, appointing and training staff in their home country and sending them overseas to manage contracts, often working in co-operation with local sub-contractors. Many such companies followed the armed forces and defence contracts and were centred around airports, naval bases and army camps. Others specialised in the oil industry and were concerned with the development of the Middle East from the 1920s onwards. Yet others became concerned with activities connected with the global mining industries and were involved in roads and railways and bridging and harbour contracts, wherever the extractive industries were to be found.

In the post-World War II global boom years of the 1950s and 1960s there were jobs for all, and many companies expanded into areas of work and regions of the world in which they had limited or no previous experience. The ending of the colonial empires in Asia and Africa broke down some of the previous special relationships, which had existed between individual colonial governments' Works Departments and contractors and consultants from the metropolitan power. The coming of political independence often led to an increase in competition in such markets with American, Italian and French consultants and contractors tendering for and obtaining work, in what had previously been secure British markets.

The existence of 'tied aid', linking a consortium of national engineering and construction contractors back to the aid agency or bank of a particular donor country, became of critical importance in obtaining work in many Third World countries. Thus the bidders for such contracts had to develop new skills in lobbying aid agencies and increasing new groupings of banks, consultants and various engineering and contracting companies to seek and obtain major new project work overseas. The availability of funds from the World Bank and other related bodies also became an important feature underpinning commercial success.

The political and governmental stability of the countries in which the work was being undertaken came into prominence as did the ever-changing relationships between the host country of the work underway, and the parent country of the principal contractors concerned. In the Middle East, Asia and Africa contracting companies frequently found themselves deeply enmeshed in the political and social milieu. Thus the international managers of engineering and construction consultants and consortia had to become as much diplomats as anything else in dealing with the day-to-day exigencies of life 'on the ground'. The OPEC years of the 1970s and the changing fortunes of the oil-producing states in the 1980s, also created the need for continuous global flexibility and adaptability on the part of the industry. In much of the 1970s the Middle Eastern oil-producing states were awash with money and the problem was one of responding to almost limitless demands for almost any type of work from the needs of the oil industry itself, to huge public construction programmes and the building of private palaces for sheiks and their families.

In the meantime, Western European home demands for construction work, centred on the needs of North Sea oil, also produced growth. For some Western Europeans other opportunities were opened up by the expansion of Eastern European and Russian requirements for extending their oil and gas industries — often leading to political controversy with American parent companies and with the US government itself.

However, with the subsequent peaking and then spectacular collapse of the price of oil in the 1980s much of this type of activity disappeared and much surplus capacity has been apparent in the industry throughout the Western world.

Throughout this story of boom and bust the development of new practices and procedures for global and country market assessments has been of central importance to the continued survival of large-scale internationally-organised engineering and construction capabilities. The industry by its very nature is intensely cyclical, living with and on the ups and downs of national business cycles which, throughout most of the post-war years, have been subject to strong government attempts, both to promote a long-term pattern of growth, and to regulate and smooth out short-term fluctuations.

However, the large-scale nature of much modern engineering, construction and consultancy capabilities inevitably has meant that it needs to extend beyond national boundaries into widespread and diverse global market situations. The extension abroad brings the promise of huge demands and growth at one moment of time and in one location, to be followed later by the threat of over-capacity and collapse. Keeping such organisations afloat and economically and technically viable has become an international juggling act, calling for enormous management capability, both in foreseeing the future and in being in the right place at the right time — and out of the wrong places at the right time as well! The fluctuating financial and economic fortunes of different parts of the world and the need for international groups to cope with such changes has underlain much of the concern about analysing the circumstances of countries and regions of the world *accurately*. It has also been the spur for creating the right mix of money resources and people skills to take advantage of those markets which become available.

In many parts of the developing world the reality of political instability and civil war has gone hand-in-hand with the continuation of major engineering and construction projects. In fact many overseas contractors have carried on working through large projects whilst surrounded by truly chaotic political, economic and social conditions. Clearly, much depends on where the investment funds supporting the project are coming from. In some cases these have been paid directly by the funding agency, such as the World Bank, directly to the home country of the contractor, thereby avoiding the many risks of sending funds to the government or the banking system of a country beset by civil war and other problems. Again, the location of the project in question is also important. It is obviously much easier for an overseas contractor to operate near a large port, which is open to international traffic, than up-country in a violence-prone, unstable political situation.

Another important factor is, which department of the host country government is the overseas contractor actually working for? For instance, port authorities or the armed forces often have a better hold on scarce foreign funds needed for overseas contracts or strategic supplies, than other departments such as roads, education or health. Thus from the viewpoint of the overseas contractor, whether or not he wishes to take on the risks of involvement may come down to such highly important questions as:

(i) Where and by what route is the money coming from to finance the project?
(ii) What local or international laws apply to the payment?
(iii) Will company's plant, equipment or works be physically close to risky, war-affected situations?
(iv) Is it possible to use the prospect of future 'tied aid' funds from Britain or elsewhere as a lever to ensure payment for the present work?
(v) Is the location of the project likely to present high or low risks to company personnel?

In terms of the risks involved, contractors often claim that their personnel are in less physical danger working in a specified construction site in a politically unstable Third World country than they are in crossing the road or walking through the park in central New York or London.

4.11 Comparing Risk in One Country to Another

There are many ways of comparing the risks of living and working and undertaking business and contracts in one country or another. Much clearly depends on the nature of the involvement and its likely duration.

In-and-out, 'tied-aid' construction projects or consultancy assignments are one thing. Entirely different are the circumstances of a long-term capital investment in a local factory, distribution and marketing network, which will take years to pay off. Financial newspapers, banking and trade journals often published lists of 'Countries in trouble' ranging from hyper risk to low risk and covering a range of political, military, economic and social issues. Yet the fact remains that many Western construction and trading companies still find it possible to operate in so-called high risk countries like Iraq, Ethiopia, Iran, Sudan and Zaire. While the risk may be very great, presumably the calculation is that sooner or later, and preferably sooner, conditions will stabilise and immense opportunities will exist for those already established in the local economy. Having lived through the bad times in company with the local people can be a wonderful base for growth once the good times return. In this process, joint venture local partners in such countries can be an enormous help in living and working through good times and bad times.

Some Management Questions

We have decided to begin to export overseas for the first time:

1. Why are we considering exporting at this time?

2. What facts do we need to start with?

3. Where do we go to obtain this information?

4. Who can help us gather these facts, either at home or overseas?

5. Which country or countries would it be best to start with?

6. How soon will we consider moving from simply exporting to seeking local agents or joint venture partners overseas?

7. Are we planning at some stage to move into establishing manufacturing capacity overseas on a joint venture or solely owned basis?

8. What will be the financial implications for the company in moving from exporting to local manufacturing and processing?

9. What are the management development and training needs of the proposed developments?

5

The Management of International Trade and Exports

The diverse and continuously changing nature of international business conditions has been outlined in previous chapters. Managers in multinational companies are continuously involved in decision-making about selling and marketing, trading and investing, joint venturing and manufacturing goods and providing services in many different markets. The possibilities extend over an enormous range of circumstances from, on the one hand, open and increasingly integrated global financial and commodity markets to, at the other extreme, government-regulated or monopolistic markets for such products as drugs and pharmaceuticals. For the export manager, a clear understanding of market environments and structures, in both a theoretical and a practical sense, is essential. It is only through such awareness that managers will be able to comprehend the differences underlying markets and to devise and operate appropriate and effective strategies and policies, geared to widely different marketing needs.

5.1 Market Structures and Government Policies

There is no world-wide general consensus as to the extent to which individual sovereign national government, or trade groupings of such nations, can or should use their many possible legal and regulatory powers to influence market conditions, either generally or specifically, in relation to goods or services.

(a) Looking first at the market demand side, in all the Western industrial economies there are widespread and continuing debates about the effectiveness or otherwise of *demand management* policies. Much of the macro-economic discussion on the demand and financial aspects of modern industrially-based economies was associated with statistical and mathematical techniques of forecasting the performance of national economies as a whole. Governments today seek to reconcile high rates of national economic growth with full employment and price stability, within an environment of reasonable balance-of-payments stability.

As we have seen, throughout the post-World War II era the influence of the International Monetary Fund (IMF) and the General Agreement on Tariffs and Trade (GATT) greatly facilitated the re-introduction of world-wide free trade outside the Soviet-led COMECON bloc. Within Britain, the challenge of operating a free trade international economy and of reconciling the external balance-of-payments problems with internal employment and growth needs shaped much of the post-war era. In the management of the US economy, balance-of-payments constraints only came into prominence following the Vietnam war inflationary pressures of the 1960s and the OPEC price rises of the 1970s. Neo-Keynesian economists on both sides of the Atlantic also became involved in prolonged debates with the 'monetarists', notably represented by Professor Milton Friedman, who are concerned with the effects of interventionist demand and employment policies on inflation, and on the traditional role of money as a store of value.

(b) Other market debates arose out of the longer-term restructuring of the *supply side of economies*, and involved consideration of questions traditionally regarded as *micro-economics*. The availability of adequate skilled labour; of savings and capital investment ratios; of materials sources and energy supplies; of management resources, etc., are all in dispute. Indicative government-focussed planning, as developed in France as part of her post-World War II modernisation plans, was seen by many as an essential partner to demand management planning in many facets of industrial life.

In Britain during the 1960s and 1970s the extension of the National Economic Development Office's Sector Working Parties, proposals for planning agreements between major companies and the government, and the heightened importance of wages, prices and incomes policies, were all put forward as a way towards assisting the more effective functioning of the industrial and commercial sides of the economy. Together with the great size of the public sector, from the nationalised industries to welfare programmes, many of which do not function in a free price system, the move towards a more 'corporatist' state seemed inevitable. Yet from 1979 onwards, a Conservative government has placed much greater emphasis on market freedom in terms of both international and national policies. Thus, in 1980 Britain moved away from foreign exchange controls and embarked on a 'privatisation' policy at home. It also sought to reduce the extent of government involvement in many other aspects of economic life.

5.2 Market Theories and Practices

Much of modern economic theory is concerned with the *micro* aspects of price determination by firms within competitive or monopolistic markets. This developed from the work of the nineteenth-century 'marginal utility' school, with the costs of the factors of production explaining the forces of supply, and the utility of the goods to the consumer their demand. The demand curve for an individual firm's products, its *average revenue* (AR) curve, is assumed to slope downwards from left to right. A steep vertical slope indicates a low demand elasticity, i.e. a change in price will not lead to a significant change in the quantity demanded. On the other hand, a flattening, horizontal average-revenue curve means that a small reduction in price will lead to a large increase in the volume demanded in the market. Likewise, on the supply side, the individual firm's supply curve or *total cost curve* (TCC) slopes upwards; the steeper and more vertical the slope, the higher the marginal cost of producing each additional unit of output.

Marketing organisation falls into two broad categories:

(a) In a state of pure or perfect competition, such as commonly applies in global currency and financial markets, and in internationally-based commodity markets for foodstuffs and minerals, there are assumed to be:
   (i) a large number of buyers and sellers;
   (ii) free entry for new buyers and sellers into the market;
   (iii) products are homogeneous, e.g. as in bulk minerals, basic commodities, or currencies;

(iv) all operators in the market have perfect knowledge of overall conditions and prices;
(v) there is generally free mobility in and out of the market of all factors of production, i.e. labour is available at a freely determined wage; capital is available at a freely determined interest rate; raw materials, management, and research and development skills, etc. are also freely available;
(vi) no artificial transport costs or barriers prevent the free movement of buyers or sellers or their products to or from the markets in question.

(b) In the state of imperfect or monopolistic competition, there is assumed to be:
(i) continuing competition among buyers;
(ii) economic rationality to maximise profits — by entrepreneurs operating within the market;
(iii) restrictions on entry by new producers or suppliers;
(iv) a falling demand or average revenue curve.

The steeper the slope of a firm's average revenue curve, the greater degree of monopoly it is assumed to enjoy. A totally vertical average revenue curve would suggest that the producer has a total monopoly, and could charge any price he wished for his product.

5.3   The Equilibrium of a Company within the Market

In economic theory, the individual company's *marginal revenue* (MR) is the income at any level of output which it will earn by selling an additional unit of output. Likewise, the *marginal cost* (MC) is the cost incurred by supplying the additional unit of output. Equilibrium for the company is achieved when marginal cost equals marginal revenue. It is assumed that the normal profit is included within its marginal cost.

For instance, if a company is operating in a highly competitive global commodity market, its average revenue curve will be horizontal and elastic. Any price change upwards would mean that it would immediately lose sales to other buyers. However, in an imperfectly competitive or monopolistic situation, its average revenue curve would be steeper and less elastic, and it would be able to adjust prices upwards without significantly affecting sales volume.

In the modern industrial mixed economies, some degree of monopolistic competition applies in many markets. This means that most products, such as industrial goods, machine tools, motor vehicles, household consumer goods, foodstuffs, package holidays, banking and insurance services are all differentiated by brand names, but that entry into these branded differentiated markets by alternative suppliers is still possible. Companies engage in considerable advertising and product promotional activities. The principal aim of the competitive monopolist is to preserve as much of his market share as possible, and to sustain existing products in their life cycles for as long as possible. However, at the same time industries as a whole may often suffer from surplus capacity, and will tend to operate at less than optimum capacity. Non-price competition will usually be an important feature of the way the market actually functions.

On the supply side, an individual company's *average fixed costs* (AFC) tend to fall as volume rises because such costs as rates, insurance, maintenance, and to some extent research and development and management skills, are spread over larger sales volumes. *Average variable costs* (AVC), which include basic raw materials, fuel and possibly labour, may also fall as volume increases. But beyond a certain point they will tend to rise as relative scarcities increase, for with increased demand such material costs, fuel and labour rates will be pushed up. The result is that the company's *total costs* (TC) rise as relative scarcities increase.

Clearly, much depends upon the nature of the industry as to when this cost rise will actually occur.

In many advanced, globally market-orientated industries economies of scale from volume manufacturing are enormous, and for very long periods of time costs may tend to fall as volume increases. Individual companies, by expanding output, will be able to take advantage of both internal and external economies. Internally, labour costs can be spread more efficiently over higher volumes of output by productivity increases. Much of the contemporary debate about the efficiency of manufacturing industry is how to increase labour productivity. The same may also apply to management, marketing and technical skills. Externally, also, higher volumes of output frequently enable firms to adopt more competitive global purchasing policies for material inputs, etc., which for a time can reduce costs of output.

Thus, internationally-based companies may be able to reduce average costs of production per unit of output for long periods of time. This particularly applies in the case of volume producers of bulk goods such as chemicals, bricks, cement, steel, and also many consumer goods, including motor vehicles, enjoying both large economies of scale and expanding market shares. However, in the long run any company's average costs are assumed to rise as the 'law of diminishing returns' eventually applies. From time to time new inventions, technology, etc. allow average costs to fall. But ultimately diminishing returns apply.

5.4 Value Adding and Profits

The questions of value adding through the production of goods and provision of services, and the earning of profit have been much debated in economic theory. Some economists have regarded profit as simply a surplus over costs of production to enable future output to be afforded — an essential return to the investor over and above what can be earned by placing the money on secure deposit with a bank or in dated government securities. Others have regarded the key role of profit as a reward for successful risk-taking. In economic theory, *normal profit* (NP) will be earned by individual companies, and by industry as a whole, when there is total market stability. It is assumed to be a level of profit which enables the industry to function continually, with a stable size of market and number of firms. In practice, in the contemporary world of global competition impacting on many products, such stability is hard to come by. However, *abnormal* or *excess* profits may be earned by a particular firm or industry which develops some unique product or a monopoly position for any one of a number of reasons. In the longer term, it is assumed that the conditions of competition listed above will eventually ensure a return to normal profits. Likewise, *sub-normal* profits, or losses, may be earned in the event of a slump in total demand. Normal profit will again be possible when the number of producers in an industry or trade has been adjusted to the new market circumstances.

5.5 Looking Ahead and Forecasting

A particular problem for much of modern, globally based industry, given the scale of manufacturing and markets involved, is how to look ahead and make sensible forecasts of market conditions. Broadly, this may be done in three ways:

(a) Management may plan forward on the basis of the type of quantitative trends in costs and prices which have obtained in the past. The further ahead the projection is made, the more *quantitative* data will need to be qualified by other *qualitative* information. In many cases companies will be producing many products, moving through different phases of their product life cycles. It will be necessary to adjust forecasts in the light of what is assumed to be the future life cycle of the various products concerned.

(b) Management may take a broad look at the ups and downs of overall cyclical activity affecting the world and national economies as a whole. For much of the post-war Keynesian era national economic demand management has sought to smooth out business trade cycles. It has promoted a service industry of consultants, forecasters and others who look at overall activity, and then seek to apply its implications to the needs of individual firms. Forecasts of this sort are as good or as bad as the assumptions and judgements of the people involved. Many firms throughout the expansive growth phase of the late 1950s and early 1960s assumed that high rates of growth would go on forever for their particular industries and trades. The lower growth 1970s and early 1980s and the impact of inflationary pressures on costs and prices made many of their longer-term forecasts downright misleading or even catastrophic in real terms.

(c) Management may simply operate on a shorter-term basis, making marginal adjustments with various *contingency* plans available to cover a range of anticipated possible events. This type of approach would no doubt be followed by companies operating in highly competitive global markets for currency, financial services or commodities. In such circumstances it is assumed that no individual buyer or seller will be able to control market forces, though from time to time unforeseen events, from new technological and scientific advances, to swings in market needs and preferences, will give temporary advantage to some producers or consumers. Flexibility of response capability is the keynote of successful management in these circumstances.

5.6   Pricing and Price Discrimination

Some examples of market organisation are indicated in the following table:

Market Conditions	With Homogeneous Products	With Differentiated Products
1. An industry with many firms	Perfectly competitive conditions are assumed to apply when there are: (a) large numbers of buyers and sellers; (b) homogeneous products; (c) perfectly free entry for buyers and sellers; (d) perfect knowledge of all those in the market; (e) free mobility of the factors of production; (f) no transport costs. A firm will be able to establish an equilibrium in the longer run and normal profits will be possible for all firms in the industry.	Monopolistic competition is assumed to apply when: (a) there is competition among buyers; (b) there are limitations on entry of new producers; (c) there is economic rationality by entrepreneurs to maximise profits. In such markets the average revenue and marginal revenue curves of the firm are always falling. The degree of 'monopoly' enjoyed is indicated by the steepness of the firm's average revenue curve. The marginal costs of firms may be rising, falling or constant.
2. An industry with a few firms	Duopoly or oligopoly with homogeneous goods In these circumstances price levels may range anywhere between pure monopoly prices and perfectly competitive prices	Duopoly or oligopoly with product differentiation In these circumstances much depends on the size, security and financial reserves of the firms in the market. There is a threat of constant competition and even war between them, but in general they desire peace and stability. Oligopolists often enter into market sharing arrangements, to spread capacity.
3. An industry with one firm	Monopolistic market The degree of monopoly established by the monopolist is the steepness of its average revenue curve and the degree of monopoly profit it is able to earn.	

Discrimination within markets may be possible owing to:

(a) consumer preferences;
(b) differentiated goods;
(c) differences because of distances or frontier barriers.

Advertising

Advertisements may be to inform the market about products or to promise their sales. When advertising to increase sales revenue, this may be done by reducing demand elasticity and thus enabling higher prices to be charged, or increasing the volume of goods demanded and thereby shifting the firm's average revenue curve to the right.

Price discrimination is assumed to apply between the prices of goods and services in different markets according to the elasticity of demand in each. For instance, a multinational company supplying many diverse *national* markets would seek to charge what each separate market would bear. It will almost certainly be involved with complex transfer pricing arrangements seeking to optimise returns in low tax areas. Price discrimination is possible when a producer is a monopolist or when there is collusion amongst sellers to discriminate on prices. Again, customers may not be able to move from one market to another, to buy in one and re-sell in the other. But when there are many sellers, consumers will tend to transfer from one to the other, to go where they can buy more cheaply. However, the same commodity may still be sold at different prices where consumers do not know that others are getting it more cheaply. Such discrimination often occurs in the sale of direct personal services because they cannot be re-sold.

Distance, involving costs of transport and frontier barriers such as tariffs, is also a reason for the existence of separate markets for the same commodity. The monopolist may take advantage of the protection offered by a tariff to sell at a higher price in the home market, but in the international market his price will be lower because he is faced with competition from many other sellers. Such price discrimination is only profitable when conditions of demand in the markets are different. If the elasticity in demand in the two markets is identical, the monopolist will not find it profitable to charge different prices. A unit of output produced at a given cost, transferred from one market to another will result in lost revenue in the first market equal to the increased revenue in the second, so there is no advantage. However, if the elasticities in demand differ, the monopolist will be able to charge more where the demand is less elastic and less where it is more elastic, till the changes in revenues in both markets equal each other, in the marginal cost of producing the final commodity or service.

In practice, most markets for industrial and company consumer goods and services are imperfect. A corporate manager will need to be clear as to pricing objectives, the time span, and the level of profits for which his/her firm is looking, what sort of markets they are seeking to create, and how these objectives relate one to the other. He or she will also need to know a great deal about total markets and the competitive situation applying to comparable or similar goods. Government policies influencing markets and prices may also be an important consideration. Likewise, cost information relating to the structure of costs within the company at different levels of output for different groups of products will also be critical.

5.7 Cost Contribution and Market Information

For managers setting selling prices, especially to overseas markets, the concept of contribution to costs is important. Firms may be prepared to price for some export markets on a marginal cost basis. Providing that the marginal or variable costs of supplying a particular export market are covered, any additional contribution a firm can get which contributes to profit, and assists with the covering of fixed overhead costs of manufacture, will be worth having. Up-to-date market information is critical. An exporter needs to have a fairly accurate idea of the degree of demand elasticity which applies to his products in particular markets. He needs to know what effect a reduction or an increase in his export prices will have on the quantities demanded. If the firm is selling in competition with a limited number of competitors, it will also need to be able to assess the effect of its price changes on competitive prices. Information about market size and shares, and their potential growth, is also important.

5.8 Flexible Currency, Exchange Rates, and Export Pricing

Throughout the 1970s and 80s British export managers had to learn how to contend with the ups and downs of sterling *vis-à-vis* other major trading currencies. Pricing for home and export markets is now decisively influenced by *floating exchange rates*, which affect the exporters' sterling prices in overseas markets and their competitive relationship to prices set by overseas competitors in their own currency, in the same markets. Firms exporting from Britain usually have more competitors in overseas markets than they do at home. This is especially true in the case of consumer durable goods, where price competition may become fierce with any slowing of growth in world markets. In the case of industrial goods, exporters may well be in an oligopolistic market, in which there is only a limited number of buyers and sellers, and a traditional system of 'orderly marketing'.

It is hardly surprising that many firms tended to regard overseas markets as being difficult, and often only made major efforts at exporting when the home market was depressed. For many British companies, exporting was often regarded as an anti-cyclical activity, and a way of spreading productive capacity and risks over several market areas, which expand and contract at different times. However, from the mid-1970s on, European and other overseas competitors entered British home markets in strength and pushed up import penetration to a level which threatened the future market security of hitherto secure local manufacturers.

5.9 Management Decision-making Options in Export Pricing

In making decisions about prices, a basic issue is whether the selling price is the key variable to be considered. Floating exchange rates may mean that price adjustments are frequently necessary. In a study of devaluation and pricing decisions based on a survey of UK companies (Hague *et al.* 1974), the authors emphasised the importance of knowing who is responsible for making such adjustments and who will be accountable for such decisions as are made. For instance, during much of the 1970s and at times in the 1980s, a British exporter could have responded to the *devaluation* of sterling against the other major trading currencies in three different ways:

(a) He might have agreed to hold foreign prices in all markets and hopefully earn a larger surplus in sterling terms;

(b) He might have agreed to reduce foreign prices in all markets, in line with the devaluation of sterling, and possibly go for an increase in volume;

(c) He could adjust prices in each of a number of markets, depending on the demand and supply position which is thought to prevail at particular periods of time.

The essential point was to adopt the right policy, that would allow the firm to optimise the return on its capital employed both in the present and also in the longer term.

During much of the 1980s, the sharp *appreciation* of sterling as a petro-backed currency has caused concern, especially to producers whose products are susceptible to price competitors and are highly volume dependent — from bulk chemicals to motor cars and bicycles. Given the international market challenges which a strong appreciation of sterling was considered to offer, the question arises of how much extra marketing and sales promotion expenditure is necessary to hold market share. This in turn raises the question of what is the company's market strategy and pricing policy in the markets under review. For instance, does it wish to retain the existing volume at a reduced unit selling price, or accept a lower volume at a higher unit selling price?

Much clearly depends on the structure of fixed and variable costs which apply. In respect to cost, it is worth bearing in mind that changes in sterling against other major currencies will also gradually feed through into the costs of manufacturing in Britain. One then has to consider how long this feed-through will take and what proportion of these raw material cost changes needs to be taken into account in setting export prices. Moreover, for many manufacturers the possibilities of substitution of different types of materials would also need to be explored, in the light of the possible fall of input prices. However, for many companies the inflation of wage costs feeding through into total costs has been the major issue of concern.

5.10   Essential Contingency Plans for Export Marketing

Given the world of floating currency exchange rates, and uncertain markets, the following points are of particular importance in setting a sound pricing and marketing strategy for export marketing. An *ongoing contingency plan* should ensure that:

(a) Management decisions are not unduly rushed, and are taken in a reasoned fashion.

(b) This implies that exporters should regularly review and assess the situation in their major markets before making decisions.

(c) Exporters should also look to the possible opportunities which a gradual *devaluation* or *appreciation* of sterling presents in marketing terms, i.e. in some circumstances they should look at export prices in terms of variable or marginal income, rather than related to average unit costs, and they should think in terms of the contribution to profits which is possible in the changing market circumstances.

(d) Exporters should not become confused by various 'political' ideas about what the 'national interest' may be thought to require.

(e) Pressure from customers and competitors should also be avoided, and exporters should be careful to avoid being stampeded by appreciation of the currency into cutting prices unnecessarily. Likewise, a currency depreciation is not necessarily an occasion for pushing up prices.

(f) If a continued appreciation of sterling *vis-à-vis* the other major currencies appears likely, exporters should consider setting their export prices in a stable or depreciating currency as opposed to setting them in sterling. Alternatively, other plans may become necessary if sterling depreciates against other major currencies.

(g) Finally, exporters and importers should as much as possible avoid unecessary *currency risks* and speculation by buying and selling their international financial needs forward, through the money market system. In recent times numerous sophisticated financial arrangements have been devised to assist exporters with their global financing and payments needs.

5.11   Successful and Less Successful Exporters

Finally, the following table taken from the British Overseas Trade Board's occasional paper, prepared by Graham Bannock and Associates in 1986, suggests the key issues for success or failure in export ventures.

What Makes for Successful Exporting

Profiles of attitudes of successful and less successful exporters: Key issues

	Successful	*Less successful*
Finding right distributors	Regard this as *the* prime issue. Board director involvement in vetting	Respond to inquiries. Expect to be found easily via directories, embassies, etc.
Commitment to export	Regard exporting as inevitable and necessary in growing business. Persistent, professional and go forward to their customers. Concern of whole company.	Insular, unprofessional, unaware of issues. Exporting seen as solution to problem of part of company only.
Learn by doing	Assume responsibility for building in-house expertise on the whole process of exporting. Automatically assume mistakes will be made.	Overwhelmed by early obstacles and blame others. Defeatist.
Selectivity in markets	Ranking process according to rational criteria, progressive focus.	Spread effort too thinly, go for high cost/risk markets too soon, e.g. France, US. Restrict efforts to passive response to unsolicited inquiries.
Financial investment	Prepared to look at projected returns on long-term basis.	Exporting seen as gamble with spare cash. Short-term view.
Long-term horizon	Several years effort necessary to lay foundations for solid success. Expect hiccoughs.	Expect quick results with meagre resources.
Confidence	Do not export until confident of success. Control growth.	Start too soon in haphazard way. Take on too much.
Respect for customer	Assume the customer will be at least as good a businessman as you are. Careful study of his needs and sensitivity to them.	Adopt take it or leave it attitude. Underestimate the customer.
Attitudes to intermediaries	Use advisers at start of export process, but thereafter only very selectively.	Either over- or under-rely on external advice. Insufficient range of potential advice sought.
Fast communications	Use telephone, fax, telex, electronic mail as appropriate.	Rely on letters. Unaware of importance of speed of response.

Less important issues

	Successful	*Less successful*
Languages	Simply part of looking after the customer. Normal in-house skill.	Over-estimate importance leading to excessive timidity or ignore altogether.
Credit risk	Regard as worse than domestic in general. Use of ECGD, Letter of Credit, proper investigation, etc. Obvious exceptions (some LDCs).	Fear of risk prevents action.
Export documentation and procedures	No problem to professionals. Handled expertly in-house or by forwarding agent externally.	Lack of professional approach: try to cut corners.
Export pricing	Accept that market determines the price; exporter has to control costs. Quote in foreign currency where customer requires it. Hedge if necessary. Aware of volume/unit cost relationships.	Inflexible attitude. Try to price at UK levels plus freight. Worry about currency problems.
Export staff recruitment	Good people can be trained in-house.	Believe good people are very difficult to find and prohibitively expensive.
Technical standards/ Legal systems	Can be a non-tariff barrier but usually surmountable.	Over-estimate importance.
Organisation of export function	May have separate export organisation or not, but whole company committed to export. Usually separate staff handle detailed documentation.	Exporting not integrated sufficiently with total business.
Payment delays	Generally similar or better than UK. Some exceptions (LDCs).	Believed to be a high cost of exporting.

Source: The Bannock Report: Bringing More Manufacturers into Active Exporting, BOTB, October 1986.

6

Living and Working with Different Cultures

6.1 Some Introductory Concepts

The main interest in the subject of cross-cultural management stems from people, who by the nature of their work are constantly engaged in working with or through cultures other than their own. These will obviously include overseas managers of multinational companies, people on secondment from their parent company to a company in another culture or country, and also the many managers who these days work in joint venture operations, both with companies and countries with which they were not previously familiar. Yet another category comprises those people who are managing organisations within their home culture, but where the nature of their work puts them in day-to-day contact with people from diverse cultural backgrounds. In contemporary Britain this includes many managers and professionals in the National Health Service, who are dealing with both patients and work-forces drawn from different cultures. Also in this category are administrators and teachers in the education system, officers in local government, the police and fire services.

The increased cultural mixture in the domestic life of many countries with the recent arrival of new ethnic minority groups, has caused a number of universities to develop a strong interest in the subject of cultural relationships. A number of universities have institutes of Community Studies which are concerned with the question of how we live with, work with, and manage more effectively with, people from countries and of cultures other than our own.

What is the minimum knowledge that we need to have to help us be more effective when working and living with people whose cultures are other than our own? Certainly a basic requirement is to know thyself and to have some understanding of what cultural patterns mean. The composition of any culture may be classified in a number of different ways embracing language, religion, values and attitudes, education, social organisation, technology, politics, law: these form the central core of ideas around which people organise their own cultural awareness. We take in many of these things from a very early age, almost, one might say, with our mother's milk, and they are deep rooted in our subconscious mind. Indeed, it is only when we meet people from cultures other than our own that we start to question why they have different ideas, values and patterns of behaviour from our own; often, it is also when we begin to think analytically about what it means to belong to our own culture. In the case of somebody from the British Isles, what does it mean to be 'British', or a regional member of that culture? What does it mean to be Irish or Scottish or Welsh; a Yorkshireman, or a Cornishman, or a member of some other regional or social grouping?

This awareness takes us forward to the problem of stereotypes. We all have pre-conceived ideas of how other people look and behave. Thus many people coming to the British Isles for the first time are immediately looking out for city gents with bowler hats and umbrellas and dark suits or cheerful Cockneys with flat caps and a line of banter or chatter. These stereotypes have frequently been projected by films, television and books about life in Britain, often rooted in the past.

Indeed, English literature, from Geoffrey Chaucer to William Shakespeare, Charles Dickens and J.B. Priestley has developed a rich and immense variety of literary stereotypes, identifiable both by regional background and by social classification. Actors, who are projecting such roles, become skilled in projecting particular stereotypes. Indeed the profession of a 'character actor' who specialises in a particular stereotype can be much more secure than that of an actor who fails to develop a stereotype. This in turn brings us forward to thoughts about what sort of 'cultural baggage' we carry in our minds about people from both our own and other cultures. What is our idea of the past, the present or even the future, and how do notions of past influences, such as imperialism, or colonialism, religion and politics and the impact of the way we learnt the language, influence our views of a culture today?

Yet another category of thinking might be shaped not so much by the national or regional culture that we are thinking about, but rather by the cultural atmosphere of a particular organisation, which is reflected both by its internal ways of behaviour and by the persona it projects, consciously or unconsciously, to the world at large.

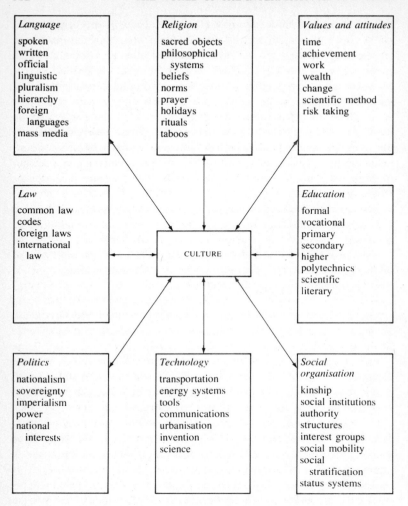

Figure 6.1 The Composition of Culture

In order to examine and analyse cultural behaviour and business, the American Professor H. Perlmutter suggested an interesting theory of business organisations which start as essentially *ethnocentric*, that is, based on a particular home culture, be it that of the USA, Britain, France or some other country. They then become more culturally universal or *polycentric*, and may eventually develop into being totally *geocentric*, having a life of their own which is increasingly detached from any clear cultural links to a particular nation or region. These categories may then be viewed against the context of socio-technical design. However, in doing this one needs to guard against stereotyping as all these characteristics may be found within the same organisation.

Another very important aspect of culture is clearly language, and the way we are trained to listen and understand. Many authorities believe that it is impossible to work effectively among other cultures without a sound grasp of the language. With this reasoning, international management training would inevitably have to include learning the relevant language.

Linking into language are the very important categories of religion and ideology, and these in turn take us forward to values and attitudes about such matters as the use of time and of distributions of wealth, the appropriate roles for men and women, the desirability or otherwise of taking risks, the importance of individual self-expression, as opposed to collective group behaviour, and the ways in which we carry forward feelings about the past, to influence the present and the future.

Indeed, all of our emotions, both in an individual and a collective sense are shaped by past or present experience. How we use that experience to shape a new future is very much a culturally-specific activity. Some cultures such as that in California favour dynamism and change for what is expected to be a better future. Other cultures, such as in much of India, powerfully influenced by the Hindu religion and civilisation, give more emphasis to the need for stability of past mores and values.

Other categorisations that also influence our view of cultures include the role of the law and the view of rules and behaviour which laws embody. British law is very much based on tradition and case law, which are capable of re-interpretation and continuous adaptation by judges. In the making of laws Parliament is sovereign, and we do not have the legal force of a written constitution. However, in other cultures people lay great emphasis on the importance of a written constitution and the interpretation of that constitution by the law. This, in turn, lays down clear central guide-lines as to the conduct of society. Part of Britain's problems of entering the EEC has centred around the fact that other European nations regard laws and regulations as much more immutable and fixed than is true in the case of British tradition. British law is capable of change both by the flexible system of case law, and also by Acts of Parliament which may be passed at any time.

Other aspects of inter-cultural understanding involve an awareness of different systems and values of education. This, in turn, often involves us in an understanding of the relationship between education for religious or academic reasons, and education or training to undertake specific tasks. Learning to get jobs through the possession of the right diplomas and degrees as opposed to actually doing jobs effectively by the exercise of real skills influences the educational systems and purpose of many countries.

Other manifestations of different cultural attitudes appear in the type of political system we enjoy; whether we lay emphasis on free will, choice, and individualism, or on a more pre-ordained and collective set of values and systems. This will affect our sense of hierarchy and reflect the 'power distance' that a society expresses through its politics. In some countries the power distance between the top and the bottom is extremely great. The gap between those in the Kremlin and the masses of the Russian people is very wide, notwithstanding the long-term espousal by the leaders of the Soviet Union of the ultimate desirability of pure Communism as a societal goal.

On the other hand, in individualistic and more democratic countries such as Australia and Canada there is a more even social hierarchy. Social values of egalitarianism demand that there be little distance between the governed and the governing.

Other manifestations of culture are also reflected in the type of artifacts and technology which we customarily use. Americans coming to Britain or Europe often complain about the obsolete technology of heating or washing, which still exists in many dwellings. Likewise, European visitors to America are sometimes confused at first by the complex technology of the American kitchen and home. Adjusting to different levels of technology is often difficult and time and patience are required for cultural adjustment.

6.2   The Use of Sensitivity Training

Various attempts have been made, both within international companies and by outside organisations, such as Farnham Castle — The Centre for International Briefing located in Farnham in Surrey — to assist with adjustment to new cultures and countries. The purpose here is to improve the quality of cultural adjustments required on overseas postings and this is done by specific training programmes. Farnham Castle has developed, over many years, elaborate training procedures taking husbands and wives together to learn about new cultures, and gives them up to a week of briefing to prepare them for the challenges that await them overseas. Farnham Castle believes that there are information needs to help one to adapt to the inevitable *culture shock* of going abroad to a strange culture for the first time; there are also some skills which can be developed to help with the process of adjustment. They also recognise that people go abroad for many different reasons and this in turn reflects their own idea of themselves, of their role in their own culture and the place that they may take up in another culture.

One feature which Farnham Castle and other such organisations have drawn attention to is what they decribe as a 'curve of adjustment' (see Figure 6.2). They have noticed that in many cases, when a husband and wife team go to live and work in a new culture, the husband often experiences a strong sense of immediate elation and achievement, and for the first few months may well have a strong sense of having adjusted successfully. However, in time he may well run into a serious loss of morale as the difficulties of the new position become more apparent to him, and it will take some time after this for him to reach an equilibrium level.

On the other hand wives, particularly those burdened with young children, moved to a strange culture, often cut off from their friends and familiar conditions, may from the outset experience a very strong sense of deprivation and loss of morale, which opens up a very significant gap between themselves and their spouses. At this stage the marriage may enter a phase of instability and it is not unknown for wives and children to depart for home without the husband and father. This is emotionally distressing and may also lead to expensive relocation problems for individuals and companies alike. In time, with some luck and help by learning and doing, the family hopefully will adjust to a more usual equilibrium level. However, experience suggests that it is an important phenomenon that husband and wife teams sent abroad may well experience different phases of culture-shock and different adjustment needs, and it is as well to recognise this as a significant problem from the outset. Those who have had experience of going abroad and living and working in new cultures, both on an individual and on a family basis, will certainly recognise the practical force of these arguments.

For these reasons over the years Farnham Castle has developed a strong system of one-week briefing programmes to prepare husband and wife teams generally nominated by the companies to go out to strange new

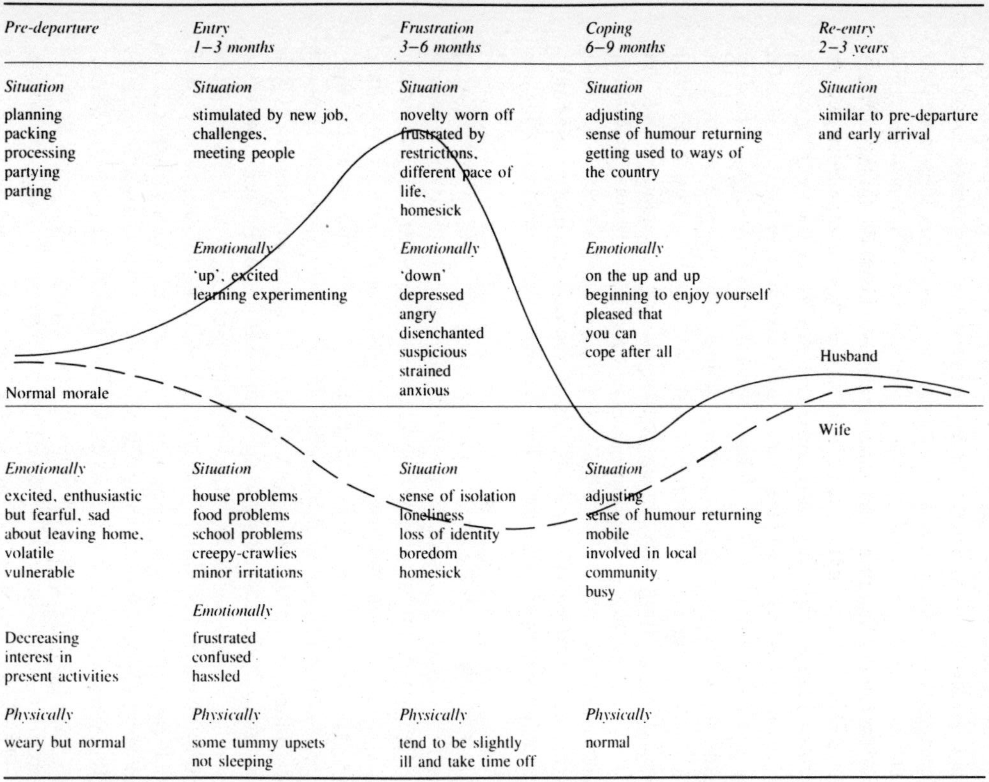

	Pre-departure	Entry 1–3 months	Frustration 3–6 months	Coping 6–9 months	Re-entry 2–3 years
Husband					
Situation	planning packing processing partying parting	stimulated by new job, challenges, meeting people	novelty worn off frustrated by restrictions. different pace of life. homesick	adjusting sense of humour returning getting used to ways of the country	similar to pre-departure and early arrival
Emotionally		'up', excited learning experimenting	'down' depressed angry disenchanted suspicious strained anxious	on the up and up beginning to enjoy yourself pleased that you can cope after all	
Wife					
Situation		house problems food problems school problems creepy-crawlies minor irritations	sense of isolation loneliness loss of identity boredom homesick	adjusting sense of humour returning mobile involved in local community busy	
Emotionally	excited, enthusiastic but fearful. sad about leaving home. volatile vulnerable	frustrated confused hassled			
	Decreasing interest in present activities				
Physically	weary but normal	some tummy upsets not sleeping	tend to be slightly ill and take time off	normal	

Normal morale

Source: Furnham Castle Centre for International Briefing

Figure 6.2 Adjustment Curves on Going Abroad

environments. Part of the strength of Farnham Castle is the wide network of contacts and speakers it has built up, who can cover most parts of the world in briefing sessions. A related strength is the ongoing maintenance and use of a Resources Centre. This is a combination of library, video and film sources and the repository of continuous flows of new global and local information in the form of letters from past students and press cuttings covering most potential situations.

The following list given to the author by M. Derhalli, Deputy Director and Course Co-ordinator for Regional Courses, gives a clear picture of the objectives and procedure followed on such week-long briefings for overseas service programmes.

Objectives

To develop
A capacity to adapt to local conditions *swiftly* and *successfully*
A sympathetic understanding of cultural values and characteristics of local
    people
An ability to gain respect and confidence of local host countries and people
An improved potential for work effectiveness

Courses
Residential
Five days long
Informal approach
Intensive
Cater for needs of accompanying wives
Cater for specific destinations
Organised on regional basis
Frequency: 9 per region, approximately 40 per year
              : once every 5 or 6 weeks
Rely on export outside speakers
Supported by well-equipped Resources Centre and
Discussions with visitors: expatriate evening
                            : national evening

Course programme design

Considerations
To cover
Each destination
Professional needs
Individual needs/interests
Needs of wives and family

The Registration Form
Clarification of interests
Clarification of previous experience
Clarification of specific needs

Maximum flexibility during programme
Use of resources at will
Optional sessions
Responding to needs as they arise

Basic elements of each course

1. *Understanding the region and its diversity*
   Historical factors
   Geo-political factors
   Economic factors
   The future

2. *Individual countries*
   The people
   Cultural background
   National institutions
   Religion

3. *How to work effectively*
   Business climate
   Industrial relations
   Government policies
   Attitudes to foreigners

4. *Social and domestic matters and social behaviour*
   Food   Health
   Housing   Recreational facilities, etc.
   Shopping   Courtesies and conventions of behaviour

Programme inputs

Staff
Experience of living and working abroad and running a household
Not specialist speakers

Outside speakers
Authoritative knowledge
Current and up-to-date
(academics; journalists; businessmen; London's proximity an advantage)

Visitors
Expatriates, recently returned
Nationals of countries of destination
50—70 speakers and visitors

The Resources Centre
Audio visual material
Documentation (on country basis)
pamphlets; paper clippings; letters; interviews
Access at will (open all hours)
Incorporated audio visual material in the programme

The Programme

FIRST DAY :

Welcome
Ice-breaking session
Introductions
Clarification and articulation of personal objectives
(what members want to get out of the course)

Introductory sessions
Visual introduction to countries
Countries are put in their regional context

SECOND DAY ONWARDS : COUNTRY DESTINATIONS
(what the course member wants to know)
Small groups, therefore virtually private tutoring

FINALE: Pulling threads together
Last use of Resources Centre
Future of region
Feed-back (collective)

FOLLOW-UP: Contact with members

6.3   Some Motives and Skills for Adjusting Elsewhere

It used to be said that Britons went to the Colonies for one of three motives — God if they were a missionary, gold if they were a trader or explorer, and glory if they were a soldier. Certainly, people still go abroad for money, or to escape unemployment or under-employment at home.

Others may go abroad for the adventure and challenge. Yet others may go abroad because they have a strong religious, or cultural impulse, which they wish to express in a new environment. Whatever the motives may be for venturing into other countries and cultures, it is clear that some people can do this with more facility than others. A listing of such skills or attributes might suggest the following broad categories that help an individual adjust to a new culture:

(a) A tolerance of ambiguity and a willingness to take on alternative goals;

(b) A low goal or task orientation, which enables the individual to be flexible in response to different circumstances;

(c) An open-minded and non-judgemental view of life;

(d) Empathy, i.e. the skill of understanding other peoples' positions and values;

(e) The ability to communicate which probably involves skill at languages;

(f) Curiosity;

(g) Sense of humour;

(h) Self-reliance.

Finally, some authorities lay great emphasis on the *ability to fail*. This means that people who set very clear goals and find failure difficult may well collapse under the pressure of trying to adjust to a new and strange culture. However, people who have developed the ability to cope with failure can, after the initial adjustment, bounce back and gradually establish a new basis of relationships with a culture they are seeking to work within.

From an international management view-point, one of the difficulties of these types of categorisations is that they suggest a fluid, flexible, open personality, who may be good at living and working in strange circumstances, or with diverse cultures. On the other hand, this sort of personality is not necessarily linked to the ability to get things done quickly. Yet one of the very qualities that 'trouble-shooting' global managers are often expected to demonstrate is high-task orientation and short-term job effectiveness. Thus, in selecting people to go abroad, companies often find they are in an ambiguous situation. There is conflict between the requirement to send somebody who will get the job done, while at the same time recognising that those with such forceful qualities may well find it difficult to adjust to new and strange cultural circumstances, with disastrous and expensive consequences for all concerned.

Various basic personality tests have been suggested as a means by which managers can be assisted to better self-knowledge and also as a way of helping them to adjust to new and strange circumstances. These tests seek to highlight different attitudes or styles of personality. They include the *factual* approach, with a strong concern and awareness of establishing the facts about situations; the *intuitive* approach, which is more concerned with instincts and emotional responses; an *analytical* approach, which looks at problems in a scientific and predictive way; and a *normative* approach, which is concerned with establishing the correct values of behaviour or procedures before moving forward to action. Most managers have a blend of these attributes and values but clearly their strongest traits do influence the way they respond to new circumstances or cultures.

Again, many commentators believe that cultures or nations themselves interpret these attributes differently from each other. They therefore take on different meanings for managerial practices and effectiveness in various parts of the world.

An interesting application of 'culture' shows that a person's underlying assumptions about 'life style', his/her personal beliefs and aspirations, inter-personal skills and relationships and place in the social structure all have a decisive influence on management performance. These cultural factors affect human values and habits relating to many key issues, from concepts of time, to ideas of duty and responsibility, to the importance of family responsibilities and to determinants of social status. These, in turn, have a powerful impact on how local employees, as opposed to the 'alien-culture' imported expatriate manager, will feel about all manner of local issues. More importantly, these will eventually affect approaches to many aspects of management decision-making and personnel policies.

6.4 Hofstede's Ideas on Organisational Design

The Dutch academic Geert Hofstede is one of the leading authorities on the cultural factors that influence both organisational design and the behaviour of those people within different organisations which themselves operate within diverse cultures and countries. For a general discussion see Hofstede (1980).

Hofstede and others have suggested that *ethnocentric* nationally-based companies inevitably run into serious managerial problems when they become multinationals because of the basic differences in the various national cultures involved. Culture, in this sense, is defined as 'the collective programming of the mind' distinguishing one group of humans from another. Thus collective differences in mental programming and attitudes exist between people from different organisations, so justifying the concept of different organisational cultures. Differences of this kind also inevitably exist among people of diverse social classes, religions, occupations, generations, sexes, geographic regions, nations, etc.

Culture as we have seen embraces values: what we like and dislike, and what we feel to be good or bad, right or wrong. Not everyone in the same cultural group will hold similar views but, statistically, the members of one cultural group will have more similar values than the members of another group, or behave in a certain way.acceptable to the group they most closely identify with. Thus, in Hofstede's words 'The British almost never shake hands; the French shake hands all the time. Eastern European and Middle Eastern men will greet other men with a kiss but never women; American men will greet women with a kiss but never other men', etc.

In a study of matched samples of people from over fifty different countries Hofstede compared their basic values. He found that these values varied in relation to four fundamental conditions in human societies:

(a) *Power distance*   How a society deals with the fact that people are unequal in a social and status sense, and how different societies deal with this reality in various ways.

(b) *Uncertainty avoidance*   How society copes with uncertainty about the future, and deals with the reality of risk.

(c) *Individualism versus collectivism*   This relates to the closeness of the relationship between one person and other persons, and raises some of the most fundamental philosophical debates about the motivations of individuals and the organisation of a society as a whole.

(d) *Masculinity versus femininity*   This relates to the division of roles between the sexes in a society, and the extent to which a society allows overlap between the roles of men and women. It impinges on the values which society places on the sexes.

Let us consider in somewhat greater detail how these categories might be applied by managers living and working overseas.

Hofstede first suggests that it is vitally important to understand the relative importance of 'power distance' and 'uncertainty avoidance' when structuring a business or similar organisation to work well in a particular country. Thus, while nature creates inequalities in our physical and intellectual capacities, human societies add to these differences and inequalities of power and wealth. Thus 'large power-distance societies' stress inequalities and develop systems in which everybody knows where he stands. Conversely, 'small power-distance societies' regard social inequality as undesirable and try to reduce it. For comparisons between societies, Hofstede developed a scale running from 0 (small power distance) to 100 (large power distance).

Clearly, societies associated with large power-distance will exhibit a high degree of centralisation of political authority and autocratic leadership. It has been suggested that this may reflect a psychological need for dependence by people without power. More likely factors, however, range from the imbalance of natural resources to the political instability and greed and ruthlessness of those in power. Asian, African and Latin American countries have high power-distance scores, whilst the USA, contemporary Germany, Scandinavia, the Netherlands, Britain, Ireland, New Zealand, Canada and Australia score fairly low in this sense.

Concerning uncertainties and risks about the future, 'Weak uncertainty-avoidance societies' encourage people to accept this uncertainty, to accept what the day brings, and to take risks rather easily. Such people can tolerate behaviour, values and opinions different from their own and do not feel threatened by them. But 'strong uncertainty-avoidance societies' teach their people to try to anticipate the future, and create institutions to establish security and stability and to avoid risk. Such security can be established by technology, laws and religion (or an equivalent dogma or ideology), often to the extent of one religion not tolerating others. Sometimes in such societies one finds a religion claiming absolute truth or a scientific tradition seeking absolute truths, giving certainty and powers of prediction over future events.

Thus 'strong uncertain-avoidance societies' include Latin-European and Latin-American countries, Japan and Korea. In Europe, Germany, Austria and Switzerland score fairly high, with Nordic countries, Britain, Ireland and the Netherlands scoring lower. Other Asian countries and African countries have medium to low scores in this respect.

How can multinational organisations effectively operate in different countries, bearing in mind that they have strong cultures within themselves? The following table plots the 'power-distance index' horizontally and the 'uncertainty-avoidance index' vertically. This can help us understand how organisations operate in different countries, since organising involves answering two questions:

(a) Who decides what? (the issues of power distributon);
(b) How can we make the outcomes predictable? (the issue of uncertainty avoidance).

By grouping fifty countries in four quadrants, Hofstede sums up his results as follows:

Index scores	Typical countries	Symbolic organisation and characteristics
Power-distance large Uncertainty-avoidance strong	Latin-European; Latin-American; Japan; Korea; Arab countries	'Pyramid of people'; hierarchical unity of command; rules
Power-distance small	Germany; Switzerland, Austria; Israel	'Well-oiled machine'; rules settle everything
Power-distance large Uncertainty-avoidance weak	African and Asian countries (except Japan and Korea)	'Family'; undisputed personal authority of father—leader; few formal rules
Power-distance small Uncertainty-avoidance weak	Nordic and Anglo-Saxon; Jamaica	'Village market'; no decisive hierarchy; flexible rules; problems solved by negotiation

The results point to some of the major differences between countries in their nationals' expectations of what an organisation should be like, and to some of the difficulties which a national ethnocentric enterprise might encounter when going multinational.

'Collectivism' and 'individualism' are part of the jargon of modern politics. Hofstede, however, emphasises in his analysis that 'collectivism' is not regarded in any political sense, and that in an individualistic society everybody is supposed to look after his own self-interest and the interests of his immediate family. This is made possible by the large amount of freedom left by society to individuals. In collectivist societies, people are born into collectives or in-groups, which may be their extended family, their tribe or their village. In such a culture everybody is supposed to look after the interest of their in-group, and the in-group in turn will protect them in times of difficulty.

Linking the differing ideas of collectivism and individualism with power-distance, Hofstede suggested that typical collectivist countries had large or medium power-distances: Latin America, West Africa, East Africa, Arab countries, Indonesia, Malaysia and Singapore. (Other evidence might suggest that some people in contemporary Singapore are distinctly individualistic.) Individualist countries, like France and other Latin-European countries, showed large power-distances, whereas Denmark, Ireland, Norway, Britain, USA, Australia and the Netherlands showed small power-distances.

In collectivist societies, there is usually a strong moral relationship between the employee and employer, the obligations being mutual. This contrasts with the relationship in an individualist society where an employee can always go off and look for better conditions elsewhere. Likewise within the values of a collectivist society, relationships come before tasks: thus in business dealings, relatives and friends should be treated better than strangers. In contrast, in business dealings in an individualist society, all people are expected to be treated equally, and tasks come before relationships.

Although, biologically, the only activities determined by the sex of a person are those related to procreation, social sex roles vary between countries. Thus in 'masculine' societies men dominate, and deal with 'things' and money, and try to be competitive, rational and unemotional. In such a society the women's role includes all kinds of caring and serving, and being feminine, emotional, intuitive and modest. In 'feminine' societies, such roles might also be performed by men, and the norms are for modesty to be preferred over ambition, the quality of life to be stressed rather than achievement, leisure to be preferred to work, and the 'underdog' to the 'superman'. According to Hofstede, Japan is the most masculine country, closely followed by Germany, Austria, Switzerland, Great Britain, USA, Australia, New Zealand and Canada. In contrast, the Nordic countries and the Netherlands are more feminine. Somewhat less so, but similar in degree, are East Africa, West Africa, France, Indonesia and Singapore, while Malaysia, Pakistan and the Arab countries fall midway between masculine and feminine societies.

It is possible to be sceptical about Hofstede's findings on social sex role divisions, but familiarity with a particular culture usually enables one to find appropriate stereotype examples if one looks hard enough. Thus a number of Frenchmen have international reputations as dress designers and perfumers; most dentists in Belgium are women, but men predominate amongst Dutch dentists.

The eighteenth-century French philosopher Voltaire spoke of the 'tyranny of possessions' and the ways in which these affect society. Hofstede finds that as nations become wealthy they shift towards greater individualism, without all becoming equally individualistic. He has seen a trend over the last twenty years for power distances to be reduced in those countries where they were already low, and he perceives a greater concern for law and order and a reduction of social tolerance with rising uncertainty-avoidance. At the same time, masculine countries tend to become more masculine and the feminine countries even more feminine.

Within large business and governmental enterprises one might perceive sub-cultures within departments, divisions and branches, and these may be hard to change if long-established. Conversely, the adoption of a new technology by an enterprise may be associated with the employment of new kinds of employee, bringing with them a very different type of culture. Mergers and takeovers create similar problems, especially if they involve enterprises in different countries, where social habits and expectations are very different. 'Hard-nosed' American approaches to business may go down well in California, but flop badly if applied in Ireland or New Zealand. However, some cultures do work together well.

Thus the Anglo–Dutch enterprises of Shell and Unilever show the feasibility of multinationals where the values on power-distance, uncertainty-avoidance and individualism are very similar, and where the 'masculine' achievement orientation of the British possibly complements the 'feminine' people orientation of the Dutch. Hofstede further concludes that 'feminine' countries, like the Netherlands, tend to be successful in consultancy, servicing or helping relationships, and in

agriculture and horticulture. They may also appear to be good at developing academics fascinated by the problems of living with and managing
inter-cultural situations.

6.5   Executive Personnel Nationality Policies

A key policy for multinational enterprise is the way in which it trains
its managerial and higher technical staff personnel to respond flexibly
to local needs. International staffing policies (and the many costs
associated with them, if they don't work well) are a critical element
underpinning successful global operations by large multinational organisations. Reference has already been made to the ideas of Professor Perlmutter about international organisations falling into ethnocentric, polycentric or geocentric modes of structure, behaviour and policies. These three
classifications and extensions of them provide a useful basis for analysing internationally-based personnel staffing policies, their strengths and
their weaknesses.

Looking at the *ethnocentric* approach a number of basic problems
immediately arise.

First, given the fact that most of the managers of such organisations
will be drawn from one home country this will almost certainly mean
restricting promotion and career prospects for those locally recruited
managers who are host company nationals. They will feel that their career
opportunities are limited by the preference given to expatriates and may
well become demotivated by this fact. In many cases locally recruited
managers will simply remain with the multinational enterprise as long
as it provides them with training and opportunities not available from
local companies. Once these opportunities have been exhausted, local
managers will naturally seek new employment elsewhere.

A second problem arises from the fact that the expatriate parent company nationals who are sent out to take up appointments in overseas
locations may be slow to adapt to local circumstances. While they may
well be trained and versed in practices and procedures at home, once
they get abroad there may be a 'slow learning curve', for themselves
and their families, in the ways of the host country, and this will naturally
reflect adversely on management performance. Coming to the country
and subsidiary company as a stranger can lead to real difficulties of social
adjustment, and expatriates may also apply inappropriate policies to differing, unfamiliar local circumstances.

Third, another commonly cited problem centres around the fact that expatriate managers from the parent country are usually on considerably higher salaries than those in similar posts in many of the host countries to which they may be posted. This is certainly true in the case of managers posted from affluent western countries to third world developing countries, where average living standards are much lower. The overseas expatriate manager will almost certainly receive an enhanced salary and other allowances, both in order to afford his home base living standards while abroad and also possibly as a tax-free inducement to be there in the first place. The London-based organisation Employment Conditions Abroad Ltd (Anchor House, 15 Britten Street SW3 3TY) provides a regular service to its members and client companies on the different costs which apply to managers and their families in different capital cities and other locations world-wide. While few would deny the need for these additional salaries and allowances, the general effect is to open up and maintain a gap between the living standards enjoyed by the expatriate manager and his locally employed colleagues. Such differences provide ready grounds for grievance and conflict. Unless well handled and understood they can become a major source of local discontent and even destructive antagonism towards the multinational company's international staff.

A variant of the problem of high salaries and allowances is the suggestion that parent company nationals may become 'dulled' by these artificial conditions and lose their effectiveness or willingness to return to more challenging, and often less well paid posts at home. It is certainly true that many expatriates who have developed a taste for the good life abroad may be reluctant to return to the struggles of the head office. There is more to this than just money. Overseas appointments often offer young expatriate managers the opportunity to take on far wider and more general responsibilities than they will ever have at home. The less specialised and more open management environment in the overseas branch can look very attractive compared to the more specialised hierarchical management structures in the head offices of multinationals based in London, New York or Paris.

Clearly some young managers would prefer to remain a 'big fish in a small pond' than move back home to become a 'small fish' in what can soon prove to be a much more threatening and bigger head office pond. If promotion requires returning to head office and if this includes the loss of many of the undoubted pecuniary and non-pecuniary attractions of life overseas, then such a move can appear to be less than attractive. Yet they are common managerial staffing problems encountered in large multinational companies, who are primarily based in ethnocentric staffing and personnel policies.

Does a more *polycentric* multicentre-based management staffing policy help such international companies to escape from such dilemmas? Some obvious advantages of appointing more local managers immediately come to mind:

(a) The extensive use of host company nationals in senior local positions can do a great deal to eliminate language and other local adjustment problems. The locally recruited manager is familiar with the linguistic and cultural environment, and should be better able to understand and deal with local problems than the expatriate.

(b) Some of the most difficult issues faced by multinationals today centre around what can best be described as 'politics', with both small and large Ps. The local manager, well attuned to his own culture, should be better able both to understand local feelings about sensitive political and politicised issues, and to respond with appropriate policies.

(c) Locally appointed staff are almost certainly less expensive than expatriates and, providing they are offered good career opportunities within the company, are likely to provide the organisation with greater employment continuity, certainly at local levels.

On the other hand, there are also a number of well-known disadvantages to relying substantially on locally recruited managers. These include:

(a) The problem of gaps opening in management understanding between the parent company located in one of the metropolitan capitals and its overseas subsidiaries. Modern business, both technically and commercially, changes rapidly, and a company relying on local managers may have difficulty in keeping information and understanding flowing freely between the centre and its branches, especially when these may be on the other side of the world and headed by local managers who may be less familiar with the latest changes than those back at head office.

(b) A polycentric company structure may also create limitations in career development opportunities, both for successful managers in the parent company and also for locally recruited managers in the subsidiary companies. It may therefore be useful to try to maintain a significant movement of managerial and senior technical staff from head office to overseas branches and vice versa.

(c) In an extreme form the polycentrically organised company could degenerate into a 'federation' of independent national units, with only nominal links to corporate headquarters. While this may suit servicing organisations such as insurance groups and consultancy practices, who rely on the centre mainly for links to markets or technical advice, it could prove disastrous for more integrated technology-based multinational companies and groups, which have a strong need for tighter and more regular organisation contracts, information flows, etc.

A further possible stage of development is towards a truly *geocentric* approach in which the personnel policy aims to create a truly 'international cadre' of management and senior technical staff who can move freely around the world and service needs as they occur on the basis of 'the best person for the job'. A related advantage of the international cadre approach would be a reduction in the tendency for national identification of managers with units of the organisation. For many companies operating with global technology and in globally competitive markets the attractions of at least trying for a truly geocentric staffing policy appear to be great. But there are very real practical problems which include:

(a) Current immigration and employment laws increasingly favour local employment. Within the EEC it is easy for member nationals to move around (subject always to the constraints of language), but for much of the world job mobility has become much harder. However, the world-wide recession of the 1970s brought in its train massive unemployment and a strong push towards job protection measures in many parts of the world, and this applies to managers and skilled technicians as much as anyone else.

(b) Other difficulties of a geocentric approach are the increased salary, training and relocation costs that often go with attempts to create a truly global, mobile, managerial and senior technical-skill workforce.

(c) Such a system clearly calls for a highly effective centralised control and flexible deployment of key staff. This could lead to the provision of less flexible staffing to handle immediate local needs. Thus while in an ideal world geocentric personnel policies have attractions, in practical terms they are probably very difficult, if not impossible, to apply fully.

6.6 Expatriate Adjustment to New Environments

Thus far, we have considered some of the problems encountered by the expatriate in adjusting to new cultural environments and some of the ways in which both companies and individuals can assist themselves in this process. A basic problem arises if there is an inadequate understanding on the part of the organisation of the problems of managers and their families adjusting to new cultures, whether they be geographical, special, or organisational in scope and type.

A number of commentators have considered the personality attributes which can assist and support the overseas adjustment process. One point of departure is the extent to which the individual, through *self-orientation* can facilitate the adjustment of coming to terms with a new cultural environment. An obvious approach is to learn to enjoy local foods, to participate in local sports and develop an interest in indigenous music, culture and drama.

Expatriate communities the world over have all developed strong social groupings to take newcomers in to orientate them to and to protect them from the local scene. These expatriate clubs have good and bad influences. They can help initial adjustment but may get in the way of developing close links with the local community. For many British expatriates one of the attractions of an overseas posting is the possibility of escaping from the complexities and stresses and strains of life in contemporary urban Britain, to a simpler life centred around the more restricted but often involving life of the local Anglo-American overseas club.

For others, a posting to a new overseas environment enables them to discover new and challenging hobbies, from scuba diving in the Pacific, to hill walking in the Himalayas or social work in the slums of Calcutta.

Whatever the possibilities the important ability is one of strong *self-orientation* and the ability to organise oneself and one's family for new opportunities and interests. It is fatal for the individuals to be constantly looking back to what has been left behind. For successful local adjustment it is important to be able to look forward to new opportunities and new interests which the local environment makes possible.

It is also helpful to try to pursue a policy of *stress reduction* by keeping a diary, writing a book, learning to draw or paint and generally to develop activities and hobbies which it is possible to undertake whatever the local circumstances may be. Self-actualisation and fulfilment in this way can assist the often lonely new arrival to adjust and come to terms with wherever he/she may be. This process can in turn lead to the development of some new technical competence.

As indicated earlier, managers sent overseas generally have ready-made sets of company objectives which, in many cases, impose on them tremendous challenges of adjustment.

It is important for the manager overseas to enhance his abilities to relate well with host nationals both in business and socially. This may lead to long-standing relationships which will bring the expatriate to a closer awareness of local language and culture. In this process of familiarisation he will learn not only about the local scene but will almost certainly be forced to a great degree of self-knowledge. The challenge of drawing from within oneself new knowledge and ideas to communicate to new foreign friends is frequently a critical part of the voyage to self-discovery which people undergo when cut off from the props of their own immediate cultural background.

Certainly the new arrival from Britain will soon be questioned about aspects of British life, from foreign policy to colonialism, the Royal Family and politics, voting records, football hooligans, food and weather. He may have limited interest in or views on some of the these topics. Yet the new arrival from the half-known or unknown culture is soon expected to field questions about these and many other complex subjects as well, and it is desirable to have some preparation for this. Thus the development of 'conversation currency' as to why they are here and what their feelings and immediate impressions are, is essential for newcomers.

Later on, the acquisition of some fluency in new languages may also be important though this depends very much on local circumstances. One of the advantages, and disadvantages, of being British is that English is also the language of much of North America, Africa, the Indian sub-continent and other parts of Asia and the Far East. Thus it is all too easy for the Englishman to coast along in the belief that the host nationals want to speak English as well — and in truth they may do. However, some attempt to learn the local languages should be made and this willingness to learn to communicate in a local language is important in seeking to develop better personal contacts and associations.

One should also consider one's *level of perception* or individual awareness of things going on around one. Some people are naturally better at this than others. The skill which needs developing is the sensitivity to 'switch on' to the local scene so as to be able to understand local thought, behaviour and culture. This requires learning the local languages, reading local papers, watching the television, listening to the radio and generally communicating with people about their everyday lives and values. This heightened individual awareness and enhanced knowledge of the local scene gives the successful practitioner the ability to understand local behaviour better and to be more objective in his views of local life.

Another consideration is the ability to adjust to a different standard of living, which may be an improvement on or less satsifactory than the one left behind. In many overseas locations, particularly in developing Third World locations, there is a much closer integration between domestic and working life. Thus the manager on a major construction project may find himself responsible not only for the building work but may also take on responsibility to the local authorities for a large camp of itinerant workers and their families who are on site. The more diverse nature of many overseas posts creates quite different stresses and pressures from those at home, and such factors as health care, housing, entertainments and even food, play a larger part in the everyday preoccupations of management. Adaptable personality traits and relationship abilities of a high order are essential.

As has been emphasised throughout, numerous environment variables can influence the situation and for most people the adjustment of the family to new and strange circumstances is critical. For teenage children the opportunity of visiting their parents in foreign parts may appear to be a bonus, but in general they will need to relate back to their own culture for education and their own future careers.

Finally, what can be said to be the main corporate management issues associated with selecting managers and their families for overseas assignments or postings?

One important point is to try and avoid making short-term decisions about expatriate staffing needs. Sending managers and their families off on overseas assignments can be a traumatic experience for all concerned and hasty decisions can easily lead to the loss of key staff by resignations which are unnecessary and undesirable. Corporate management needs to make accurate forecasts of its future requirements for overseas posts. This may be easier said than done if the company finds it is operating in volatile and unpredictable global markets. The construction and contracting industry is notoriously prone to losing and gaining large projects, in distant locations, at short notice. In these circumstances, when there is insufficient time for lengthy selection and training procedures, there may be little choice but to 'roll with the punches' and to rely heavily on expensive short-term recruiting and sub-contracting.

However, multinational organisations such as international banks, insurance groups and similar bodies operate in more stable and predictable markets and, in theory at least, should be better placed to plan staffing needs both at home and overseas, well into the future. This allows adequate time for selection and training procedures.

Expatriate selection and training should begin early in career terms and go on in a regular way after this. Companies with the long-term plan to sustain a significant presence in a large number of highly competitive global markets clearly need to invest in their management and senior technical staff early on. If they don't, they may well founder or lose growth opportunities because of the lack of suitable staff with the right blend of skills, personality and languages to take on new markets as they arise.

Some Management Questions

1. Why is it necessary to send expatriates and their families overseas?

2. What criteria are we using to select or recruit people for such overseas assignments?

3. Where do we seek training assistance to prepare them to function effectively overseas?

4. What are their anticipated relationships with people already in post? Is this a new or a replacement appointment?

5. What sources of information could help our staff with the process of adjustment to new cultures and strange conditions?

6. Who seems most likely to adjust easily to overseas conditions? Alternatively, who is most likely to experience difficulties?

7. How long should managers and their families be posted to particular locations?

8. How will we measure success or failure in different countries and cultures?

9. What are the costs and benefits of sending expatriates overseas as opposed to local recruitment?

7

The Challenge of
The Developing Countries

Managers working in the post-independence developing countries of today face many difficult and complex strategic choices, challenges and opportunities. This applies whether they are working on behalf of a multinational company, in a joint venture with local partners, or as an expatriate expert or technocrat with a local company or organisation.

All these managers must have the ability to reflect on where they, their enterprises, organisations and countries have come from, where they are currently and where they can, in light of the local circumstances, realistically plan to go to in the foreseeable future. In this process political awareness and sensitivity to changing social values are of prime importance. These skills are essential qualities for those seeking to fit into an often strange and volatile business environment, with enormous elements of opportunity and risk apparent at each stage of decision making. Some understanding of the culture they are part of, and its recent history of political independence, social and industrial development, etc. is essential for the expatriate manager, who may often be regarded, rightly or wrongly, as on instrument of change.

7.1 The Inheritance of Independence

Over the last thirty years many developing countries have achieved independence. As they did so they could look back to the inheritance of their colonial period, to the existence of a basic infrastructure and of links with a mother country and with a world language, be it French, Spanish, Portuguese or English. Many institutions, established when they had been colonies, had become an integral part of their societies. The

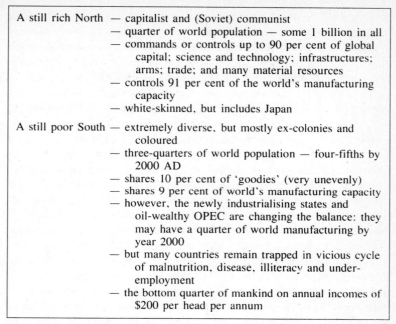

A still rich North — capitalist and (Soviet) communist
— quarter of world population — some 1 billion in all
— commands or controls up to 90 per cent of global
capital; science and technology; infrastructures;
arms; trade; and many material resources
— controls 91 per cent of the world's manufacturing
capacity
— white-skinned, but includes Japan

A still poor South — extremely diverse, but mostly ex-colonies and
coloured
— three-quarters of world population — four-fifths by
2000 AD
— shares 10 per cent of 'goodies' (very unevenly)
— shares 9 per cent of world's manufacturing capacity
— however, the newly industrialising states and
oil-wealthy OPEC are changing the balance: they
may have a quarter of world manufacturing by
year 2000
— but many countries remain trapped in vicious cycle
of malnutrition, disease, illiteracy and under-
employment
— the bottom quarter of mankind on annual incomes of
$200 per head per annum

Figure 7.1 North—South Issues for the 1990s

impact of the missionaries, both Christian and Islamic, should not be
understated.

A complexity of factors were transforming the post-war international
scene and world-wide growth presented a huge opportunity. It provided
the developing countries with a good initial base to start with. At the
same time the very success of the new prosperity and the buoyancy of
prices for primary mineral and agricultural products also created a climate
of optimism which lulled many of the leaders of the newly independent
states into a quite false euphoria as to the possibilities before them.

As has been indicated earlier the post-war era was characterised by
another important geo-political phenomenon — the emergence out of
World War II of the USA and the Soviet Union as super powers and
the rapid decline of the traditional world role of the Western European
countries. The two super powers each represented revolutionary creeds.

The United States had been based on a revolutionary escape from
eighteenth-century colonialism and an espousal of the principles of
democracy and freedom including the rights of the individual citizens

to seek life and liberty, the pursuit of property and happiness. These aspirations were enshrined in their constitution. It was also a country which nearly a century later had fought a bloody civil war which led to the emancipation of the slaves of the Southern States. Thus the United States had good credentials to present itself as a revolutionary force, firm in its commitment to combat the evils of exploitation and colonialism, but linking these with a strong belief in the ideals of one man one vote and of the importance of the free market for enterprise and economic growth.

The USSR emerged from the devastation of World War II as a major new industrial power, extending its buffer zone empire well into the heartland of Europe and anxious to promote itself as an alternative political, economic and social development model to that pursued by the capitalist West. Marxism/Leninism and Soviet ideas of central planning, together with the notion of the inevitable evolution of society through Marxist historical stages, were an important intellectual inheritance which the Soviet Union felt it had a duty to present. There can be no doubt that Marx's and Engels' original message of the evolution of society through revolutionary states, starting with primitive (tribal) communism and evolving via slavery to feudalism and capitalism and then via a further transformation to socialism and back to pure communism, but in a highly industrialised form was, and still is, a powerful revolutionary message. It gave an historical perspective of man within the cycles of inevitable historical and social change. It was attractive to many leaders in developing countries, confronted as they were with their own inheritance which they interpreted as having condemned them to a state of slavery or feudal colonialism; a colonialism that was related to the interests and whims of a distant metropolitan power which, in large part, had become highly urbanised and industrialised.

It must also be emphasised that the majority of the leaders of the newly independent developing countries had been educated at Western universities and they were deeply imbued with the aspirations of Western society. These included a belief in democracy, the rights of one man to one vote, the desirability, in some cases, of a more socially aware and socialist society and, in many cases, the assumption that Western technology and science would be comparatively easily transferred to meet the needs and expectations of their own peoples. It was probably this last point, bearing as it does on the fundamentals of social organisation, on the structure and motivations of individuals and groups and their ability to cope with changes, which presented some of the most basic difficulties of transferring ideas from the West to meet the needs of many developing countries.

The developing nations themselves represented many different stages of development and types of cultures. In Asia ancient civilisations with deep religious values such as Hinduism, Buddhism, Islam and Confucianism set particular parameters. In Africa, the impact of religious beliefs given by Catholic and Protestant missionaries was also important. Islam had also had significant successes in many parts of Africa. In Latin America, much of which had long been politically independent, but was still in many ways part of the developing world, the influence and traditions of Catholic Spain and Portugal in structuring the basis and motivations of society cannot be overlooked.

So much then for the background to post-World War II independence upon which planning for change had to proceed. A confusion of historical situations, of rapid social, political and economic changes, was compounded by confusion as to the ideals of democracy and of the way to apply these to the development needs of newly-independent, aspiring, primary-producing states. Management needs were, not surprisingly, often overlooked in the initial enthusiasm of independence.

7.2 Three Perspectives of Development

There can be no neutral theory of development since each alternative necessarily has a political dimension. Three theories may be described: laissez-faire individualism, collectivism and scientific technological change.

First is the idea of *laissez-faire*, or the free market, which came from the ideas of the English political theorist John Locke (1632–1704) and the Scottish economist Adam Smith (1723–1790). They recorded the most important priority for society as the promotion of individual and market freedom: people may wish to be socially dominant and have aspirations to join an élite; they may attribute their own pecuniary success and the economic successes of society as a whole to individual talents and hard work. This type of philosophy which, today, is vigorously supported by President Reagan in the United States and Mrs Thatcher in Britain, is politically conservative.

A second set of theories, common in many developing countries and regarded by many as deriving particularly from the ideas of Karl Marx (1818–1883), Frederick Engels (1820–1895) and to some extent Lenin (1870–1924), is *collectivist*. Society is part of a series of inevitable social changes in development and all production and consumption inevitably takes place within the social context. In this line of thought, it is not

Table 7.1 Three Perspectives of Development

Individualism, free will and choice	Historical determinism	Technology and systems management
John Locke (1632−1704) and Adam Smith (1723−1790)	Karl Marx (1818−1883) and Friedrich Engels (1820−1895) Vladimir Ilyich Lenin (1870−1924)	J.M. Keynes (1883−1946) Demand Management
Nineteenth-century capitalism	Evolution through revolution (a) Primitive communism (b) Slavery	Supply side management
Twentieth-century mixed economies and welfare states	(c) Feudalism (d) Capitalism (e) Socialism (f) Pure communism	Soviet central planning
		The possibility of détente and convergence between competitive political and social systems
OECD industrial states	Chinese agrarian society COMECON industrial states	

so much what productive decisions are taken, but who takes them. Productive resources are regarded as a social asset and ought to be under the control of society as a whole, through some form of governmental or social representation. In the Western world many of these ideas became part of socialist thinking and were often thought of as being socially radical or revolutionary. However, in the developing countries a collectivist view of social development and economic activity often equated more easily with the traditional tribal and group dynamics, than it did with the individualistic theories espoused by supporters of *laissez-faire*.

A third set of theories owes little to the philosophising of eighteenth or nineteenth century political and economic theorists. It suggests that it is the possession and application of science and technology which is critical to the ways in which societies do, or don't, develop. Modern industrial development is essentially a matter of how much science and how much technology is available to be applied to productive purposes. This puts the promotion of development into the hands of technical specialists and experts of whatever branch of the social and natural sciences seems relevant. It asserts the supremacy of the engineer, the physicist, the agronomist and maybe even the economist, the anthropologist or the management scientist, to the problems of development. In a developing country context, the role of the 'technocrats' is certainly important. Many of these technocrats come in on highly paid expatriate short-term contracts. While in some senses they may be regarded as politically reformist force, in general they are not seen as directly challenging the prevailing power structures. Yet in many developing countries, the technical specialist who has proved to be most significant has been the soldier with the means of taking control of society. The problem is that the Generals have very little idea of what to do with the power they have taken and rely on other specialists, often economists, for advice as to what should be done.

The scientific and technocratic theories of industrial growth suggest that what really matters is the application of these branches of knowledge to the solution of problems. The naive belief is that everything is solvable provided the scientists, the engineers and the economists and managers are allowed to get on with it — hence the proliferation of consultants and overseas experts in most developing countries today.

*   *   *

By the 1950s the conflict between the interests of the West, as exemplified by the United States and her Western European allies and the interests of the Eastern bloc, as personified by the Soviet Union and her group of satellite states, had become more polarised. An assortment of new actors on the world stage was also appearing. These included the emergence of China who had a period of flirtation with the Soviet Union and then a phase of going it alone. Also in the Far East, newly industrialising states such as Japan were soon to be followed by South Korea, Taiwan, Hong Kong and Singapore and, in the Middle East, Iran and Egypt and many others were coming onto the scene. There was seen to be an urgent need to try to reconcile different philosophies of development.

One of the most interesting and influential development debates was stimulated in the late fifties through the publication by Professor W.W. Rostow (1959) of his book *The Stages of Economic Growth — a Non-Communist Manifesto*. These ideas originally appeared in the pages of the London *Economist* and were seen as a way of linking together Marx's idea of historical stages, but they point to ways in which society could have social progress and economic development without engaging in the violence of Marxist-style revolutions.

Rostow suggested that society could develop from two early stages, traditional primitive society and pre-conditions for 'take-off': these stages were pre-scientific and ones in which actions were conditioned by tradition and culture. However, once a society took hold of modern Western technology and science it was capable of beginning to offer sophisticated divisions of labour and economies of scale in manufacturing and service industries. At this stage the countries would be able to move through a 'take-off' phase into a stage of mature industrial technology and later move to high mass consumption. In order to undertake these transformations it would be necessary for the whole of society to go through a series of complex social and political developments and, more importantly in the technical sense, to raise the *real* rate of investment from five to ten per cent. Rostow suggested that this would be more than adequate to cover the depreciation on existing stocks of capital and infrastructure and to add significantly to the total stock available to society as a whole. Both capitalist and Marxist-influenced developing economies face acute problems of mobilising enough investment capital from local savings to fund industrial development. They face gaps in raising enough overseas investment capital to compensate for the inadequacy of local savings, and gaps also to deal with the costs of having adequate foreign exchange for future import needs.

Interestingly enough, when societies — capitalist or Marxist inspired — reached the point of high mass consumption, there was a tendency, according to Rostow, for real rates of economic growth to level off. He linked this levelling-off to a number of conditions. First was a tendency for such societies to have to spend more per capita on welfare expenditures. There were two reasons for this: first, that the children required longer education in order to prepare them to enter the work force and, secondly, a tendency for people to live longer, well into their 70s requiring more expenditure on health, housing, welfare, etc. This prediction (1959) has been well borne out by the experiences of all urban and

---

What distinguishes the NICs from most of the non-oil developing countries is the emphasis which they place on outward-looking growth policies as a means of promoting rapid industrialisation. This has led to a steady, and in some cases dramatic, enlargement of export market shares and of the domestic market.

Assisted by these developments, the NICs have also been able to attract foreign capital of various types which has, amongst other things, accelerated the diffusion of advanced technology in manufacturing industry.

Source: The Impact of the Newly Industrialising Countries on Production and Trade in Manufactures, OECD, Paris, 1979.

Figure 7.2 The Newly-Industrialising Countries (NICs)

Rising share of OECD imports of manufactures from NICs —	1963—2.6 per cent 1970—4.4 per cent 1977—8.1 per cent 1980s—further diverse growth of imports

Heterogeneous aspects of 10 NICs — Korea, Taiwan, Mexico, Brazil, Yugoslavia, Portugal, Hong Kong, Greece, Singapore, Spain:

- their populations range from over 2 million (Singapore) to 110 million (Brazil);
- their areas range from one thousand square kilometers (Hong Kong and Singapore) to 8.5 million square kilometers (Brazil);
- extensive mineral and agricultural wealth (Brazil, Mexico) contrasts markedly with limited natural resources (Hong Kong, Singapore, Korea and Taiwan);
- the shares of agriculture, industry, services and foreign trade vary considerably;
- nominal per capita GDP of the richest NIC (Spain) is six times that of the poorest (Korea) and slightly more than twice in real terms.

This means great diversity in their development patterns, problems and policies. However, there is the overall emphasis which they place on outward looking growth policies as a means of promoting rapid industrialisation.

Figure 7.3 Policies and Problems of the Newly-Industrialising Countries

industrial societies since then and the levels of state support both for education for the young and welfare for the aged have become two of the most persistent political problems. Citizens at both ends of the spectrum, the young, from age 18 onwards, and the old, have votes and they are becoming powerful interest groups which need to be accommodated within the goals of society as a whole.

A second Rostovian reason for a falling-off of the growth rate in per capita terms was the tendency for an increase in military expenditure. As Voltaire pointed out long ago, society is faced by a tyranny of possessions. These assets require defence, both by strengthening the forces of law and order internally and by defending the state from external threats, such as a cut-off of oil supplies or interruption of trade routes.

A third reason for the lowering of the average growth rate was the sheer difficulty of making correct investment decisions. As Marx had pointed out, one of the problems of large-scale capitalism was a tendency to invest in competitive technologies which, when faced with weaknesses of demand, often led to cut-throat competition. Modern high technology industry has had great difficulties in forecasting the needs for many forms of investment and thus there have been major errors. Power stations, petrochemical works, aeroplanes, consumer goods, etc. may have been built in quantities and to standards far beyond the eventual needs of society. Errors in investment decisions become a critical constraint on growth.

From the early 1970s onwards, other reasons for a slower rate of growth have also become manifest. The OPEC oil price rises of the 1970s, following on from the inflationary pressures of the late 1960s certainly constrained growth and created uncertainty and unstable profitability and employment in many industries.

A further reason perceived for lower rates of growth in the 1970s was deteriorating returns from new investments in key industries. Much of the technology and science which had been so important in raising productivity in the immediate post-war period had run out of steam. In order to raise productivity in the future new technologies would be necessary. Many commentators have seen the onset of computer-based systems as providing the basis of a new technological revolution in Western Society. This, of course, has profound implications not only for factory employment but also for many service industries.

Another reason for growth rates in the advanced industrial countries to fall is that they have moved into a more service-based economy, the larger element of services being in the form of health, education, take-away food convenience stores, higher levels of expenditure on holidays, insurance, etc. This type of service-based economy is simply less growth-prone in per capita economic terms than a manufacturing economy. It is less dependent on the physical growth of output of goods to sustain general activity.

7.3   Increasing the Rate of Economic Growth

Looking to the developing countries, the most important management message of Rostow's stages of economic growth is the possibility of getting nations as a whole to substantially increase living standards within present lifetimes. Yet in practice expectations of per capita growth have proved difficult to fulfil. There have been all manner of reasons for failure some of which have had little directly to do with the developing countries themselves. In the immediate post-war era the general boom in commodity prices provided a favourable environment to undertake all forms of innovation. There was simply more money to go round to introduce new ideas and new developments. The multiplier effect, spreading through the developing countries, of booming commodity prices was very real. However as the world's industrial system ran out of growth it became increasingly difficult for many developing countries to sustain their progress, dependent as they were on a few primary export products. Later the onset of inflationary pressures deriving from the Vietnam war period of the mid 1960s and going on to the OPEC oil price increases in the 1970s onwards also has had a profoundly dampening effect on growth prospects open to the non-oil producing developing countries. Their situation had become dominated by the fact that they were highly reliant on oil-based fuel products and the fact that in many cases these products had come to constitute something like half of their total import bill. Thus an unstable inflation situation combined with high world energy prices had a profound impact on the prospects facing the average person, from the town dweller to the peasant proprietor. The slowing down of growth hit people's *expectations* very hard indeed.

7.4 Development Theories and Practice

Throughout the 1950s and 1960s the main fashion was for *modernisation*: a theory which suggested that 'seek ye first the kingdom of economic growth and all things shall be added unto you' or, more crudely, that *more is better*. This approach placed great reliance on high national growth, with the international use of labour and economies of larger scale production. There was often a naive optimism about industrialisation programmes and their effects on the general prosperity of society as a whole. Import replacement and export promotion schemes proliferated. Modernisation theories generally went hand-in-hand with a rapid increase in the size of cities and growing urban employment. Rising levels of nutrition and health services, the fall of infant mortality, a tendency for people to live longer, all led to runaway population growth. Developing countries found their population increases going up 2−3 per cent per annum and these rates of increase began to erode the possibility of raising per capita incomes.

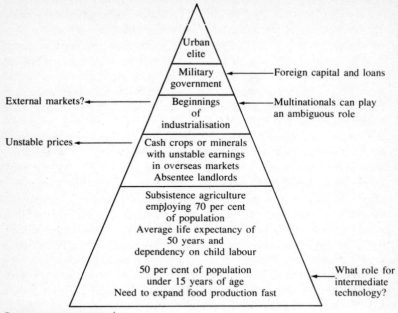

Some management questions:
1. Who provides the surplus for investment?
2. Where should the new investments go?
3. Is foreign aid a *good* thing?
4. Social and political motivation for change?

Figure 7.4 Some Management Dilemmas of a Third World Developing
Country

In the 1970s, the impact of slower world growth rates deriving particularly from the OPEC oil prices led to a new set of ideas which has
been broadly described as the *basic needs approach*. It was increasingly
recognised that economic growth in some societies had made things worse
for some of their people. Rapid growth and prosperity for the new elite,
especially for those living in towns, had not necessarily made society
as a whole better off. Gradually, in response to the new reality, governments began to give less emphasis to growth targets and to talk more
about the case for redistribution and equity.

There was an obvious inability of new industries to absorb the surplus
labour which was coming forth from the rapid growth in population.
At the same time, in many areas there was serious industrial mismanagement and real declines in productivity and output. The growth

of the cities was creating urban squalor and waste. Michael Lipton wrote an excellent book called *Why People Stay Poor* about this.

Finally, more developing countries at this time were starting to run into a serious balance of payments crisis which added to their difficulties in earning adequate foreign exchange from their traditional primary exports to cover essential imports of industrial raw materials and critical energy supplies.

During the slow-down of the 1970s other theories came forward associated with the notion of *dependency*. In this line of thinking it was increasingly suggested that national growth policies were helpless in the face of the 'unfair international order' and that the international use of labour which had worked reasonably well in the 1950s and 60s had turned out to be good for the rich countries at what was described as the centre, and bad for the developing countries on the periphery of world economic prosperity. The questions remained as to what national economic growth policies should be, and whether or not it was possible to change within the international order.

At the same time, a new breed of newly industrialising countries going through the 'take-off' phase had emerged. They were no longer solely reliant on the attractions of cheap labour. Rather, they had been able to attract to themselves significant amounts of investment from the multinational companies to invest in some of the very latest technologies and to export successfully a broadening range of consumer goods, such as rubber goods, textiles, domestic electrical appliances including radio and television, photographic equipment and motor vehicles for a wide range of markets. Indeed their success was becoming such that they were beginning to pose a serious threat to the established market positions of many of the older industrial countries of Western Europe and North America.

All of these developments were raising some basic questions which have a direct bearing on the ways a developing country, or enterprises within such an economy, are actually managed. These centre around such key national management issues as:

1. The balance-of-payment resources availability compared to levels of economic development.
2. The role of the state *vis-à-vis* the market.
3. Central state planning as opposed to private initiatives.
4. The desire for growth compared to the need for fairness and equity.
5. Centralised company decision-making as opposed to participatory management styles.

6. Whether a developing country pursues a free trading policy as opposed to a self-sufficiency policy, notwithstanding local vested interests favouring the latter.
7. The need for restructuring of basic industries.
8. The relationship between tax measures and burdens and the tendency in many countries for a large non-taxed economy to emerge.
9. The appropriate role of welfare as opposed to that of giving people an incentive to work.

In a number of the developing countries where the attempts to have rapid industrialisation had not worked and where the 'trickle-down' effect had clearly not extended very far into enhancing prosperity in the countryside, a new look was taken at the whole nature of development policies. Indeed, the philosophy of development started to shift away from a simple belief in the benefits of industrialisation and back towards restoring productivity and effectiveness of the agricultural base. This requires a balance between the claims of the rapidly growing urban areas and the needs for more rural development. It raises questions as to whether growth patterns should be market determined as opposed to politically determined and emphasises the basic need for priorities *vis-à-vis* the welfare of the individual and a simple pursuit of increasing growth per capita. Other difficult questions arise regarding capital intensity and whether a more selective use of intermediate or appropriate technologies should be adopted.

One of the most fundamental difficulties facing development has been the lack of adequately trained or motivated managers to fill the middle or senior strategic roles in enterprises. The colonial period had often left the local people woefully under-educated for anything but the simplest, almost menial tasks. A few had been educated to a very high level in academic disciplines but this had not necessarily fitted them, either intellectually or psychologically for becoming junior managers and gradually developing managerial and technical competence. It is not unusual in many developing countries to see an enormous gap between the basic peasant proprietors and those holding a variety of degrees and professional qualifications from many parts of the world. The 'diploma disease', with its propensity to train people *to get jobs* as opposed to *actually doing jobs*, has blighted many development efforts. There has often been a serious dearth of a middle management or entrepreneurial class capable of taking on the effective day-to-day running of enterprises and gradually moving through this experience into more senior management positions. The need to develop effective managers on the basis of real experience of practical problems is perhaps the most important need for development in the future.

7.5 Ways of Looking at the Enterprise

Working in a developing country forces the manager to go back to basic issues and beliefs. There are many different ways of looking at the problem of managing enterprises. The behavioural scientists tend to regard an enterprise as an organic creation looking outwards to its trading environment and inward to the skills available for continually evolving in response to new needs and new opportunities. The mathematically trained manager tends to look to the organisational need to forecast, to project forward against past and present trends into some operational view of future opportunities. The further he looks ahead the more difficult it becomes. Quantitative data has to give way to qualitative judgements. The economically and financially trained manager may well look at a business as consisting of costs and revenues and will seek to establish some optimum level of operations to optimise profitability from different plant sizes. For some enterprises the product life cycle becomes important. As one product moves through its economic life, other products must be in the pipeline to fill the gaps left by the decline of the previous product. Yet another managerial view of the enterprise would be to seek to analyse those factors which are enabling it to go forward, as opposed to those factors that are restraining or holding it back from its desired target.

In practice, managers in developing country situations need to take a number of different views. They have to be aware of the organic, creative nature of the enterprise and the possibility of it expanding or contracting in response to changing market needs. They also have to be aware of the possibilities of using financial and quantitative methods to analyse accurately costs and revenue flows and to forecast future profits. These skills require not only a basis of professional training but also, more importantly, the ability to reflect upon experience and to think *laterally* across subject boundaries in such a way as to take an integrated view of the opportunities and challenges presented to the enterprise.

To this end, a useful task is to ask managers to think about the strategic planning needs of, say, an agricultural enterprise operating in a particular developing country. They need to assess those facts about the external environment — political, governmental, economic, social, financial and technical — which present (a) opportunities or (b) threats to a proposed development. Having done this they then need to look inside the organisation, at the resources and finance, technology and people and to set about creating realistic goals for promoting growth with efficiency.

They will need to reconcile the facts about the external environment with those of the internal requirements and recognise that the organisational goal for economic and financial efficiency may also have to be reconciled with broader social responsibilities. This may present formidable management problems. The enterprise may be required by its board to maximise profits. This may suggest the need to invest in modern machinery often imported from abroad. This may well reduce employment opportunities in the area and may also increase the country's dependency on imported spare parts, raw materials and such like. In a developing country, the reconciliation of economic efficiency with broader social responsibilities is probably one of the most difficult tasks facing senior managers. It calls for a sensitive balance between, possibly conflicting, demands, locally and from head office.

In many developing countries much of the industrial/commercial sector has become or has always been part of the governmental machine. There is a tradition of bureaucracy and of top-down bureaucratic management. Orders have traditionally flowed from the top down to the bottom. Yet given the changing and diverse nature of business conditions such a rigid command and reporting structure may prove to be hopelessly rigid and inflexible in responding to changing market needs. In such circumstances there is an urgent need to encourage junior and middle managers to think actively about their roles, of the sort of plans they are required to undertake, and to think how they might seek to influence the form of strategic plans going on within their own organisations.

There is a need to encourage a more *bottom-upward* approach to thinking, building up from the grass roots of the organisation rather than simply leaving the organisation floundering along with unworkable obsolete plans imposed from above. Similar problems frequently occur in private companies which are at the end of a multinational chain of command. Ideas and directives which may appear to be sensible in New York, London or Paris may, at grassroots level in certain developing countries, be totally unrealistic.

The only way that this situation can be dealt with is to create a body of informed, capable local managers who are able to think critically and who can shape the direction of the overseas enterprise as a whole. The existence of this type of independent critical thinking on the part of an expanding group of junior and middle managers may be uncomfortable for senior managers used to issuing orders from above. But the process of wide thinking about policy choices can, of course, prove to be a major stimulus to management thinking as a whole.

7.6   Dual Economies and Stages of Market Development

Typically the poorer developing countries display characteristics which have been described as 'a dual economy' with a basis of subsistence and cash crop agriculture and also some elements of more advanced industrial and commercial activities based in urban centres. Much of the economy consists of people engaged in subsistence food production, or local market-related agricultural activities. Some have also developed plantation-type crops such as tea, cotton and sisal for export. There are also extractive industries for a variety of minerals, often located in remote rural regions.

The next stage is the growth of a simple exchange or servicing economy, moving forward to some limited low-technology manufacturing within a number of urban centres. The urban society based primarily on the functions of government and on services, displays many of the characteristics of more affluent societies. It usually embraces a relatively affluent middle class, both local and expatriate, working in administration, the professions and business, who have life styles and demands for goods and services similar to those which apply in the more developed industrial countries.

Several stages of market development will be apparent. Each of these stages requires a different style and strategy of management. At the base of the market there is a stage which might be described as being *product* or *production* orientated. It is characterised by a relative scarcity of goods and by consumer behaviour shaped by low levels of employment, income and living standards by many people. In such a market poor consumers are prepared to buy whatever is cheaply available, but it is essential that the products they can afford to buy satisfy basic needs. These include lamp-oil, cheap watches, bicycles, simple water pumps, agricultural tools, etc.

The management of local businesses which satisfy these basic needs is characterised by a belief in the importance of having good simple products. Managers assume that there is a continuing if undiscriminating

STAGE ONE OF MARKETING THINKING

Production orientation

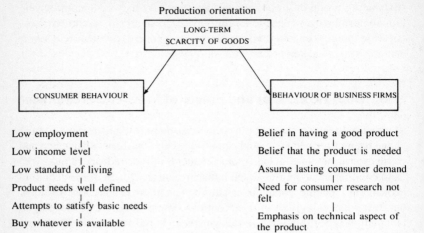

CONSUMER BEHAVIOUR	BEHAVIOUR OF BUSINESS FIRMS
Low employment	Belief in having a good product
Low income level	Belief that the product is needed
Low standard of living	Assume lasting consumer demand
Product needs well defined	Need for consumer research not felt
Attempts to satisfy basic needs	Emphasis on technical aspect of the product
Buy whatever is available	Profits through cost reduction and increased production

STAGE TWO OF MARKETING THINKING

Sales orientation

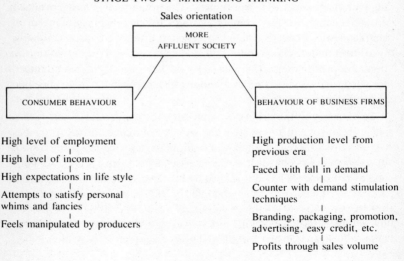

CONSUMER BEHAVIOUR	BEHAVIOUR OF BUSINESS FIRMS
High level of employment	High production level from previous era
High level of income	Faced with fall in demand
High expectations in life style	Counter with demand stimulation techniques
Attempts to satisfy personal whims and fancies	Branding, packaging, promotion, advertising, easy credit, etc.
Feels manipulated by producers	Profits through sales volume

Figure 7.5 Management in The Developing Countries

consumer demand for a limited range of cheap products, and not much research is necessary. There is generally an emphasis on the technical aspects of the product, and a belief that company profits come through cost reduction and by increasing production. However, as time goes by, and the poor rural economy develops, people often have surplus cash after satisfying their *basic needs*, and start to be more selective in their purchasing. This may lead to a fall in demand for the simple range of products, which local firms have been relying on to enlarge their production capacity. In order to maintain a high sales volume for a limited range of simple products, and to enable them to stay in business, companies are often forced to 'cut-throat' selling in order to entice consumers to buy the limited range of products which they produce locally.

Moving up the income scale in a developing country generally means moving into the more urban-based markets, which are more comparable to those in affluent, market-related economies overseas. Consumer behaviour is shaped by the reality of higher levels of regular employment and income. People have higher *expectations* of possible life styles, and wish to satisfy their personal whims and fancies. Rising real disposable incomes mean that there is an increasing demand for more sophisticated and more costly goods and services.

The management of local business firms, which are sometimes branches of multinationals, may have large stocks of basic products from the previous era, but will now run into more diverse and sophisticated market demands. Certainly in such a market, low prices become much less critical, and such features as branding and packaging, sales promotion, advertising, easy credit, etc. become more important. Profit is seen as coming both through sales volume and by enhancing the quality and the *value-added* characteristics of the goods and services on offer.

7.7 The Promotion of Small Businesses and Co-operatives

In many developing countries governments have devoted considerable time and resources promoting indigenous entrepreneurship in small enterprises which are considered appropriate to local circumstances. A useful study of the role of small businesses in developing countries is by Professor Malcolm Harper, *Small Businesses in the Third World: Guide-Lines for Practical Assistance*, which was published in association with

Intermediate Technology Publications Ltd (Harper 1984). This organisation is concerned with devising technologies appropriate to the limited circumstances of small companies in developing countries.

In many developing countries *co-operatives* also have an important role in the economy. The management of co-operatives both small and large presents basic problems for government. Because they so often fail in competition with private industry some co-operatives are primarily concerned with consumers, while others organise producers, often of agricultural produce which is sent from the country into the urban centres. A basic issue is the fostering of enterprise, innovation and change within the co-operative form of organisation. In practice, rural co-operatives generally have a special relationship with the local government. They are often used as an instrument for collecting together foodstuffs and other raw materials from the countryside, either for internal redistribution or for export overseas; and they have also been used as an instrument for levying taxes. For this, if for no other reason, local producers may have a jaundiced view of co-operatives.

7.8   Large Companies in The Public and Private Sectors

In general these may be considered to fall into the three main categories of government-owned companies sometimes known as *Parastatals*, larger *local private companies* and the subsidiaries of the multinational enterprises.

The government-owned enterprises are concerned with the monopolistic provision of such essential public services and utilities as water supplies, electricity generation, the running of urban services, railways, the harbours, docks, airports, bus services and, in some cases, banking and insurance services, etc. They have been modelled to a large extent on the nationalised industries in advanced industrial countries, and have encountered many of the managerial problems which they share. How do they balance, on the one hand, the need to run efficient, 'profitable' enterprises with, on the other hand, the political and social pressures for a wider network of essential services to service the most needy members of the community, who are often in outlying and remote rural areas?

The idea of *privatising* such government-owned enterprises may have political support and also be attractive to management. However, the Parastatals often derive from the nationalisation, following independence, of what were previously foreign-owned companies and there is a tremendous political commitment in maintaining *national* ownership and control. Moreover, in many countries there are insufficient financial resources available in the local money market to purchase such enterprises. Compared to Britain, where there is a huge private money market, with the continuous and sustained support of fresh injections of cash from savings in insurance companies and pension funds, most developing countries have very limited local private money markets. Such as exist may not be able to provide the large mobilisation of funds necessary to privatise large state owned companies, even if this was thought to be desirable for political or efficiency or other reasons. Again, in most developing countries many Parastatals are seen as a major means of providing employment to large, low-skilled urban workforces, as much as anything to do with the provision of basic services or products at competitive prices.

In addition to the Parastatal sector, in most developing countries there is a group of medium to large-sized privately or publicly-owned *local companies*. In most cases these have developed from small companies which have become larger through business success. They frequently have close links with the government and official bodies through family associations. They often rely on government purchasing and tariffs or quotas against competitive imports from overseas. They may also have partly expatriate overseas ownership and management. In many developing countries an expatriate community developed private businesses, under the support of the colonial system. In East and Central Africa for instance the Asian business community traditionally played a large role in setting up and running enterprises. Likewise in West Africa, Lebanese traders, and other expatriates, have been important in the creation of large local enterprises, in building and construction work, garages, light engineering, and the provision of a wide range of locally produced consumer goods.

7.9 Joint Ventures, Licensing and Technology Transfer Arrangements

Licensing and wholly owned subsidiaries are often used as a means for the transfer of technology from the developed to the developing countries. Joint ventures differ from licensing agreements in that licensing does not involve the sharing of equity. However, a joint venture can be structured so as to be a party to licensing, franchising, contract manufacture, industrial co-operation agreements and management contracts, as well as joint assembly and manufacturing operations. There have been many ideas as to the conditions which facilitate successful technology transfers through international joint ventures. These include the careful selection of partners and a conductive corporate structure, particularly on the part of the technical partner, who is normally based in the developed country. A high absorption capacity of such technology on the part of the local partner is also desirable, as are the ability to develop shared benefits from the venture and, of course, goodwill and commitment from the top management of both the partners.

In developing countries there have been many examples of failure to transfer technology in the way that was planned. These failures may be ascribed to many factors including unfavourable, or changing local political and economic conditions, a lack of adequate preparation underpinning the relationship, unwillingness to effect a transfer of certain technologies, lack of trust, poor management, and inappropriate technology and trading. Often bad timing and communications problems, partly caused by language barriers and cultural differences also create difficulties in joint ventures of this sort.

Under-pinning many of these relationships is the problem of deciding, not only on the joint venture itself, but on the *appropriate technology* to be transferred. Partners in developed countries frequently possess a wide range of technologies which are based on the assumption of small but highly skilled work forces. This contrasts with those simpler technologies which require large numbers of less skilled labour. Indeed sometimes technologies which have been surperseded or abandoned in an advanced industrial country might be appropriate for transfer to a developing country, which has a different mix of labour skills and availability. There are many instances of comparatively obsolete technologies being transferred from advanced industrial countries and successfully applied in the still relatively labour intensive low cost technology environment of a new host country.

The appropriateness of technology to a political or economic environment is an area of great sensitivity. Sometimes the *technical partner* in the developed country is seen as wishing to dump obsolete technology on an unwilling *host partner* in a developing country. Alternatively, the government of the developing country may be insistent that the country should receive the latest technology, irrespective of the appropriateness of the equipment and its application to their local market conditions.

National pride and honour may be involved in such attitudes and policies. Again the scale of many companies, large-scale and high-tech in the developed country partner, and smaller and low-tech in the developing country, may also inhibit effective technology transfer.

Some critics have gone so far as to say that much of modern Western technology is inappropriate to many developing countries, particularly those who have a substantial proportion of their economy at very low levels of industrialisation and urbanisation. In a labour intensive largely subsistence rural economy there may be few opportunities for effectively applying modern technologies. Thus there have been vigorous arguments that new forms of *intermediate technologies* need to be developed, which are more appropriate to the current stage of development of the developing country.

There are many ways of facilitating and managing the processes of development. Joint ventures in technology transfer, through the agency of business partners in countries at different stages of development, is one. But it can present difficult choices and challenges, both for the companies themselves and for the governments in their attempts to promote beneficial long-term economic growth and social development for the society as a whole.

Some Management Questions

1. How important is a knowledge of the developing countries to your own company's future business opportunities?

2. What business contacts do we presently have with specific developing countries and how might they be improved or extended in the future?

3. In what ways would we need to change our management ideas and practices in order to work within a specific developing country?

4. To what extent are our current management practices and technologies transferable to specific developing countries?

5. What particular types of licensing or joint venture arrangements should apply in our relationships with specific developing countries?

8

Summary and Conclusions

Throughout this introductory text several themes of both a general and a particular nature have been referred to. The basic learning need of those studying international business for the first time is to acquire a broadened outlook on the many international developments which are continually impacting on the global scene. Wide reading, listening to radio and watching television reports in a discerning and critical fashion can assist with this process. Travel and actual involvement with facets of international business and trade can also be an invaluable experience.

Chapter 1 looks at the historical background to the present-day scene. The changing patterns of industry and trade, of politics and international institutions are outlined. A distinction is drawn between those who see the future of global business being conducted on increasingly competitive lines and those who favour more protectionist and, possibly, regionally-based policies. The case of Britain within the rapidly evolving European communities highlights many such issues. Attention is given to various global scenarios of the future: demographic changes, patterns of food grain production and distribution, global energy supplies, and transfers of science and technology to newly industrialising countries. Environmental debates of many origins and types and North—South and East—West conflicts and cooperative ventures are also surveyed. Behind all of these questions lies the critical geo-political question of whether interdependence or divergence will become the future global order. All these broad-based and rapidly changing issues underlie the nature of the international business environment both today and in the foreseeable future.

In Chapter 2 we move on to consider the role of the great multinational enterprises (MNEs) in contemporary global markets. The origin and nature of these enterprises, their ownership and control, and the policies they pursue have become major fields for academic research and teaching, and also for the formulation of public policies at both international and national levels. The impact of the MNEs on investment, employment and markets in diverse parts of the world has become the subject of widespread news and political commentary. Britain, as a leading industrial nation, is both the parent of, and the recipient of, numerous internationally-based enterprises and activities. As such, it provides an ongoing case study of many of the political and social issues involved. Attention is also given to the many recent changes in world financial markets and the onset of huge and continuing money markets and financial transactions on a global basis. Computers and telecommunications have together created the possibility of a 'global village' for money in a way unforeseen even a decade or so ago.

Chapter 3 moves forward to the theme of strategic thinking and planning by the individual corporate manager caught up in rapidly changing world markets. As such managers move around the world they and their companies will inevitably encounter widely varied political, economic and social ideas. They will need to adjust corporate policies and actions to fit in with diverse local circumstances. At the same time they will also have to devise effective strategies to meet with global competition in many hitherto local markets. These types of issues are considered in four global mini case studies involving debt and development, energy resources and availabilities, armaments and security, and commodities in international trade.

In Chapters 4, 5 and 6 the text moves on to give particular attention to some facets of international business which can be used more directly to enhance individual and company effectiveness in competing in world markets. Thus Chapter 4, on the analysis of global opportunity and risk, includes sources of information and advice when looking for the first time at overseas market opportunities, and it provides three check-lists to assist the manager with this task. Reference is also made to overseas investment appraisal and the means of comparing risk in one country to another.

Chapter 5, on the management of international trade and exports, looks at many practical aspects of doing business abroad. These include analysing diverse market structures, costing and pricing in a world of floating exchange rates and of differences in attitudes between successful and less successful exporters.

Chapter 6 then moves on to the essential qualities necessary to living and working with different cultures. The need for enhancing adaptability and sensitivity by the manager, his spouse and family, is emphasised.

The need for a corporate policy to help with the process of adjustment to varying cultures and circumstances overseas is also indicated.

Chapter 7 looks at the challenge of the developing countries. This returns to many of the broad issues raised in Chapter 1 but gives particular attention to the conditions of life which apply in the immensely varied parts of the world which have been collectively labelled the Third World. In reality, a huge variety of political, economic and social circumstances apply. Nevertheless, attention is drawn to some common strands of history including the ending of colonialism and the move towards more urban and industrial ways of life. At the same time the factors of rapidly increasing populations, poverty and deprivation, especially in rural areas, remain ever present.

The theory and practice of development as it is applied in many diverse circumstances is referred to. The expatriate manager must understand the historical and social background of his new location and be able to fit his company into the local framework. Multinational companies have an important role to play in helping many developing countries provide a more prosperous and satisfactory future for their peoples. The chapter concludes with discussion of the potential contribution of new international business cooperation through joint ventures, licensing and technology transfer arrangements.

Throughout this text the need for would-be international managers (and their families) to be well prepared for living and working within the rapidly changing global business environment is emphasised. Through the processes of learning they must first seek to acquire broad awareness and ongoing interest in the changing global scene. On this basis they can then go forward to acquire the other very necessary skills of languages, cultural sensitivity, and the various business sciences and techniques which will allow them to create appropriate policies for application at local levels. The need for intellectual breadth and depth and then the ability to apply these to particular needs is what the world of the international manager is all about.

Appendix:
Global Tables

Table 1 World Population Trends (in millions)

	1500	1800	1900s	1940s	1970s	2000
World	350	1000	2000	3000	4000	6000+
Europe	60/70	190	480	540	670	700
(including Russia)						
UK	4	16	42	48	56	58

Table 2 World Population mid-1985 (000s)

WORLD TOTAL = 4,837,000

AFRICA	555 000	EUROPE	542 000
Egypt	48 503	France	55 162
Ethiopia	43 350	West Germany	61 015
Nigeria	95 198	Italy	57 128
South Africa	32 392	United Kingdom	56 618
Zaire	30 363		
		SOVIET UNION	278 618
NORTH AMERICA	401 000		
Canada	25 379	ASIA	2 768 000
United States	239 283	China (mainland)	1 040 600
		India	750 900
SOUTH AMERICA	268 000	Japan	120 754
Argentina	30 564	Pakistan	96 180
Brazil	135 564	Philippines	54 378
Colombia	28 624	Vietnam	50 713
OCEANIA	25 000		
Australia	15 752		
New Zealand	3 254		
Papua New Guinea	3 329		

Source: The Economist Diary, 1988

Table 3 World Food Grain Production — 1986 (000 tonnes)

WHEAT		BARLEY	
World	535 635	World	180 413
Soviet Union	92 300	Soviet Union	51 400
China	89 000	United States	13 292
United States	56 792	Canada	13 026
India	46 885	France	10 063
RYE		MAIZE	
World	31 785	World	483 604
Soviet Union	15 000	United States	209 632
Poland	7 179	China	64 200
East Germany	2 403	Brazil	20 512
West Germany	1 818	Romania	20 000

Table 4 Industrial Raw Materials — 1986 (000 tonnes)

COTTON		PIG IRON	
World	15 505	World	486 000
China	3 540	Soviet Union	110 000
Soviet Union	2 550	Japan	75 666
United States	2 132	China	50 092
India	1 360	United States	39 804
IRON ORE		CRUDE OIL	
World	740 000	World	2 750 000
Soviet Union	250 000	Soviet Union	615 000
China	139 562	United States	430 687
Australia	91 300	Saudi Arabia	251 000
Brazil	75 454	Mexico	140 000
COAL		CRUDE STEEL	
World	3 630 000	World	714 000
China	870 000	Soviet Union	161 000
United States	744 300	Japan	98 266
Soviet Union	631 000	United States	73 233
Poland	210 310	China	52 050
WOOL		NATURAL GAS	
World	1 791	World	1 780 000
Australia	477	Soviet Union	686 000
Soviet Union	270	United States	480 000
New Zealand	265	Canada	82 000
China	113	Netherlands	81 000

Source: The Economist Diary, 1988

Glossary:
An International ABC

Many international organisations, agreements and plans are usually referred to by a group of initials. Below is a key to some of the contractions in common use.

ASEAN (Association of South East Asian Nations)

Established in 1967, to accelerate economic growth and stability in the South-East Asian region. Members are Brunei, Indonesia, Malaysia, Philippines, Singapore and Thailand. *Headquarters*: Jakarta.

BENELUX (Benelux Economic Union)

Established in 1960, to form the economic union of its members: Belgium, Netherlands and Luxembourg. *Headquarters*: Brussels.

COMECON (Council for Mutual Economic Assistance (CMEA))

Established in 1949 to assist the economic development of its members. Members are Bulgaria, Cuba, Czechoslovakia, East Germany, Hungary, Mongolia, Poland, Romania, Soviet Union and Vietnam. *Headquarters*: Moscow.

ECOSOC (Economic and Social Council)

One of the principal organs of UN which promotes economic and social co-operation and co-ordinates the work of the specialised agencies. Membership 54.

ECSC (European Coal and Steel Community)

Established in 1951, and came into being July 25 1952 to increase efficiency in coal and steel industries by removing trade restrictions. The original six members were Belgium, France, West Germany, Italy, Luxembourg and Netherlands; Denmark, Ireland and United Kingdom joined from January 1 1973, Greece from January 1 1981 and Portugal and Spain from January 1 1986. *Headquarters*: Luxembourg.

EEC (European Economic Community)	Established in 1957 by the members of ECSC, and came into being January 1 1958 to promote economic and political activities by establishing a customs union (The Common Market). Members: as for ECSC. *Headquarters*: Brussels. (London information office: 8 Storey's Gate, SW1P 3AT).
EFTA (European Free Trade Association)	Established in 1960 to promote economic development and expansion of trade within the area. Members are Austria, Finland, Iceland, Norway, Sweden and Switzerland. The agreement also applies to Liechtenstein. *Headquarters*: Geneva.
ESCAP (Economic and Social Commission for Asia and the Pacific)	Formerly ECAFE; established by ECOSOC and reorganised in 1974. Membership 37, 8 associates (1987). *Headquarters*: Bangkok.
FAO (Food and Agriculture Organisation of the United Nations)	Specialised agency established in 1945 to advise on conservation of natural resources and methods of food processing and distribution. Membership 158 (1987). *Headquarters*: Rome.
GATT (General Agreement on Tariffs and Trade)	Signed in 1947 by 23 countries and directed towards the reduction of trade barriers. 90 contracting parties (1987). Has special association with UN. *Headquarters*: Geneva.
IAEA (International Atomic Energy Agency)	Established in 1957 to develop the peaceful uses of atomic energy. Membership 112 (1987). Has special association with UN. *Headquarters*: Vienna.
IBRD (International Bank for Reconstruction and Development)	(World Bank). Established in 1945. It guides international investment and provides loans. Membership 149 (1987). *Address*: 1818 H Street NW, Washington DC 20433.
ICAO (International Civil Aviation Organisation)	Specialised agency established in April 1947 to promote the safe and orderly development of civil aviation. Membership 156 (1987). *Headquarters*: Montreal.
ICJ (International Court of Justice)	All members of UN are parties to the statute of the Court (15 judges elected for 9 years), binding themselves to comply with its decisions in cases to which they are parties. *Headquarters*: The Hague.
IDA (International Development Association)	Specialised agency affiliated to IBRD to promote economic development. Membership 134 (1987). *Address*: at IBRD.

IFC (International Finance Corporation)

Specialised agency affiliated to IBRD to invest in productive private enterprise in developing countries. Membership 128 (1987). *Address*: as IBRD.

ILO (International Labour Organisation)

Established 1919 and now a specialised agency aiming to improve working conditions. Membership 150 (1987). *Headquarters*: Geneva.

IMO (International Maritime Organisation)

Specialised agency established in 1959 to promote co-operation on international maritime questions. Membership 127, 1 associate (1987). *Headquarters*: 4 Albert Embankment, London, SE1 7SR.

IMF (International Monetary Fund)

Specialised agency established with IBRD after the Bretton Woods Conference. It promotes foreign exchange stability to stimulate world trade and operates as a central banker. Membership 149 (1987). *Address*: 700 19th Street NW, Washington DC 20431.

ITU (International Telecommunication Union)

Formed in 1932 and now a specialised agency. Membership 160 (1987). *Headquarters*: Geneva.

NATO (North Atlantic Treaty Organisation)

Founded by 12 countries in 1949 to unite efforts for collective defence. Membership 16 (1987). *Headquarters*: Brussels.

OECD (Organisation for Economic Co-operation and Development)

Established in 1961 as a successor of OEEC (European Economic Co-operation). 19 European members, Australia, Canada, Japan, New Zealand and United States (Yugoslavia has special status). *Headquarters*: Paris.

OPEC (Organisation of the Petroleum Exporting Countries)

Established in 1969 to unify and co-ordinate members' petroleum policies. Membership 13 (1987). *Headquarters*: Vienna.

UN (United Nations)

Established on October 24 1945. Its principal organs are
(1) General Assembly of all members normally meeting once a year;
(2) Security Council of 15 members;
(3) Economic and Social Council;
(4) Trusteeship Council;
(5) International Court of Justice;
(6) Secretariat.
Membership 159 (1986). *Headquarters*: New York. (London information centre: 20 Buckingham Gate, SW1E 6LB)

UNCTAD (United Nations Conference on Trade and Development)

Established in 1964 to promote international trade. *Headquarters*: Geneva.

UNESCO (United Nations Educational, Scientific and Cultural Organisation)

Specialised agency which came into being in 1946. Membership 158, 2 associates (1987). *Headquarters*: Paris.

UNICEF (United Nations Children's Fund)

Established in 1946; provides assistance for the benefit of all children, especially those in developing countries. *Headquarters*: New York.

UNIDO (United Nations Industrial Development Organisation)

Established in 1965 to promote industry in developing countries. Membership 139 (1987). *Headquarters*: Vienna.

UPU (Universal Postal Union)

Specialised agency established in 1875 to unite members in a single postal territory. Membership 168 (1987). *Headquarters*: Berne.

WHO (World Health Organisation)

Specialised agency established in 1948 to raise standards of health. Membership 165, 1 associate (1987). *Headquarters*: Geneva.

WIPO (World Intellectual Property Organisation)

Specialised agency of the UN from December 1974; it promotes co-operation in the enforcement of international agreements on trade marks, patents, industrial designs, literary and artistic works etc. Membership 115 (1987). *Headquarters*: Geneva.

Source: The Economist Diary, 1988

Bibliography

General References

Columbia Journal of World Business.
Commodity Research Bureau Inc., *Commodity Yearbook.*
Commodity Studies Ltd, *Commodities and Financial Futures Yearbook.*
Department of Trade Journal, *British Business*, weekly.
Economist Intelligence Unit, *European Trends*, quarterly.
Economist Intelligence Unit, *The World in 1987*, annually.
European Community Law publications.
International Institute for Strategic Studies, Annual Strategic Surveys.
International Monetary Fund Annual Reports.
Journal of the Overseas Development Institute, *Development Policy Review*, Sage,
    London.
Journal of the Society for International Development, Rome, *Development.*
Journal of the Strategic Planning Society and the European Planning Federa-
    tion, *Long-Range Planning*, Aberdeen University Press, six issues per annum.
Journal of the Third World Foundation for Social and Economic Studies, London,
    Third World Quarterly.
OECD, various publications.
Royal Institute of International Affairs, *World Affairs* and *The World Today.*
United Nations Economic Commission for Europe, *Economic Bulletin for Europe.*
World Bank, *World Development Report*, United Nations, annually.
Yearbook of International Organisations, Saur, 1987.

Chapter 1

Business Blue Book (1905), Curtis Gardner and Co., London.
EEC and Barclays Bank (1988) *Europe 1992: Developing an Active Company
    Approach to the European Market*, Whurr Publishers Ltd.
Independent Commission on International Development Issues (1980)
    North/South: A Programme for Survival, Don Books.
Keynes, J.M. (1936) *General Theory of Employment Interest and Money*,
    Macmillan.
Lesourne, J. (1979) *Facing the Future, Mastering the Probable and Managing
    the Unpredictable*, Interfutures Group of the OECD.

Mayne, R. (1983) *The Dawn of Today's Europe*, Thames and Hudson.
Ricardo, D. (1817–21) *Principles of Political Economy and Taxation*.
Smith, A. (1776) *An Enquiry into the Nature and Causes of the Wealth of Nations*.
US Government (1982) *Global 2000 Report to the President*, Penguin Books.

Chapter 2

Brooke, M.Z. (1987) *International Management: A Review of Strategies and Operations*, Hutchinson Education.
Buckley, P.J. and Casson, M. (1985) *The Economic Theory of the Multinational Enterprise*, Macmillan.
Casson, M. (ed.) (1983) *The Growth of International Business*, George Allen and Unwin.
Dunning, J.H. (1958) *American Investment in British Manufacturing Industry*, George Allen and Unwin.
OECD (1977) *Guidelines for Multinational Enterprises*, Institute for International and Foreign Trade Law, Washington, DC.
Reddaway, W.D. (1968) *Effects of UK Investment Overseas*, Cambridge University Press.
Robinson, R.D. (1978) *International Business Management, 2nd edn*, The Dryden Press, Hinsdale, Illinois.
Stopford, J.M. and Turner, L. (1985) *Britain and the Multinationals*, John Wiley.
World Bank (1987) *World Development Report*, Oxford University Press.

Chapter 3

Royal Institute of International Affairs (1981) *Western Security: What has changed and what should be done*.
World Bank (1979) *World Development Report*, Oxford University Press.
World Bank (1985) *World Development Report*, Oxford University Press.

Chapter 4

Jacobsen, K.H. and Nelson, J.W. (1980) *Evaluating Uncertainties in Foreign Investment*, Stanford Research Institute, Stanford University.

Chapter 5

Bannock, G. and Associates (1986) *Bringing More Manufacturers into Active Exporting*, British Overseas Trade Board.
Hague, D.G., Oakeshott, E. and Strain, A. (1974) *Devaluation and Pricing Decisions*, George Allen and Unwin.

Chapter 6

Hofstede, G. (1980) *Cultures Consequences: International Differences in Work-related Values*, Sage.

Chapter 7

Harper, M. (1984) *Small Businesses in the Third World: Guidelines for Practical Assistance*, Intermediate Technology Publications Ltd and John Wiley and Sons.

Hutton, J. (1979) *The Mystery of Wealth: Political Economy — Its Development and Impact on World Events*, Stanley Thornes (Publishers) Ltd.

OECD (1979) *The Impact of the Newly Industrialising Countries on Production and Trade in Manufactures*, Paris.

Rostow, W.W. (1960) *The Stages of Economic Growth — A Non-Communist Manifesto*, Cambridge University Press.

Index